Teddy's Button

Teddy's Button

By
Amy Le Feuvre

(Author of *Dwell Deep, Eric's Good News,*
Probable Sons, and *Legend Led*)

"His banner over me was love."

Contents

CHAPTER I

AN ANTAGONIST

He stood in the centre of a little crowd of village boys; his golden head was bare in the blazing sun, but the crop of curls seemed thick enough to protect him from its rays, and he was far too engrossed in his occupation to heed any discomfort from the heat.

A slim delicate little lad, with a finely cut face, and blue eyes that by turns would sparkle with animation, and then settle into a dreamy wistfulness, with a deep far-away look in them. They were dancing and flashing with excitement now, and his whole frame was quivering with enthusiasm; with head thrown back, and tongue, hand, and foot all in motion, he seemed to have his audience completely spell-bound, and they listened with open eyes and mouths to his oration.

With one hand he was fingering a large brass button, which figured conspicuously in the centre of his small waistcoat, and this button was the subject of his theme.

"My father he rushed forward—'Come on, men; we'll save the old colours!' And they shouted, 'Hurrah!'

as they made after him. There were guns going, and shells flying, and swords flashing and hacking away, and the enemy poured on with fiery red faces and gnashing teeth! My father drew his sword—and no one could stand against him, no one! He cut and he slashed, and heads and arms and legs rolled off as quick as lightning, one after the other. He got up to the colours, and with a shout he plunged his sword right through the body of the enemy who had stolen them! The enemy fell stone dead. My father seized the colours and looked around. He was alone! The other soldiers had been beaten back. But was he afraid? No. He gave a loud 'Hurrah!' picked up his sword, and fought his way back, the enemy hard after him. It was a race for life, and he ran backward the whole way; he wasn't going to turn his back to the enemy. He pressed on, shouting 'Hurrah!' until he got to his own side again, and then he reached his colonel.

"'Captain dead, Sir! I've got the colours!' He saluted as he said it, and then dropped dead himself at the colonel's feet, the blood gushing out of his heart, and over his clothes, and over this button!"

The little orator paused as he sank his voice to a tragic whisper; then raising it again, he added triumphantly, "And thirty bullets and six swords had gone through my father's body! That was something like a soldier!"

"Oh, I say!" murmured a small sceptic from the crowd, "it was twenty bullets last time; make it fifty,

Teddy!"

"And that's the story of my button," pursued the boy, ignoring with scorn this last remark.

"And did your father have only one button to his coat?"

The voice was a strange one, and the boys turned around to meet the curious gaze of a sturdy little damsel, who had, unnoticed, joined the group. She was not dressed as an ordinary village child, but in a little rough serge sailor suit, with a large hat to match, set well back on a quantity of loose, dark hair. A rosy-cheeked square-set little figure she was, and her brown eyes, fringed with long black lashes, looked straight at Teddy with something of defiance and scorn in their glance.

Though at first a little taken aback, Teddy rose to the occasion.

"One button!" he said with emphasis. "The coat was sent to Mother with only one button left on; and if you—" here he turned upon his questioner with a little fierceness—"if you had been through such a bloody battle, and killed so many men, you would have burst and lost all your buttons, and not had one left, like Father!"

There was a round of applause at this, but the small maiden remained undaunted.

"Is that a true story you told?" she demanded, with severity in her tone.

"Of course it's true," was the indignant shout of all.

"Then I tell you, Boy, I don't believe a word of it!" And with set determined lips she turned on her heel and walked away, having sown seeds of anger and resentment in more than one boyish breast.

"Who is she?" asked Teddy as, tired and exhausted by his recital, he threw himself on the grass to rest.

One of the bigger boys answered him. "I saw her come yesterday in a cab from the town to old Sol at the turnpike—she and her mother, I reckon. They had two carpetbags and a box and a polly parrot in a cage. I counted them myself, for I was having a ride behind, and the woman called Sol 'Father,' so the little one must be his granddaughter!"

"Perhaps they've come from America," suggested a small urchin, capering around on his hands and feet. "Parrots always come over the sea, you know."

"She didn't believe me," murmured Teddy, chewing a wisp of grass meditatively.

"Gals are never any good! If she had been a boy you would have fought her, but I shouldn't care for anything like her, Ted."

Teddy turned his face upward to the speaker. "No, I couldn't have fought her, Sam, if she had been a boy. I've promised my mother I won't fight again until she lets me. You see, I fought four boys in one week last time, and she says she won't have it. I don't see that if it is right for soldiers to fight, why isn't it right for boys?"

"I don't think there are any fellows left for you to fight with, so you are pretty safe. Besides, it was only Tom Larken, who set them on to try and get your button from you, and he has gone off to another part of the country now."

"I think, perhaps," went on Teddy slowly, as he turned over on his back and looked up at the clear, blue sky above him, "that I wasn't quite true about the bullets. I think it was six bullets and three sword cuts. I forget when I tell it how many it was; but she said she didn't believe a word!"

Five o'clock struck by the old church clock close by. Teddy was on his feet in an instant, and with a wild whoop and shout he was scudding across the green, his curls flying in the wind, and his little feet hardly seeming to touch the ground.

There was none in the village as quick-footed as Teddy, and for daring feats and downright pluck he held the foremost place. Perhaps this accounted for his popularity. Perhaps it was his marvelous aptitude for telling stories, many of them wild productions from his fertile brain, but certain it was that he was the pet and the darling of the village, and none as yet had resisted his sway.

Over the green, up a shady lane, across two fields, and then, breathless and panting, Teddy paused before an old-fashioned farmhouse. He passed his hands lightly through his curls, pulled himself up with a jerk, and then quietly and sedately opened a latched door and entered the long low-roofed kitchen.

There was something very restful in the scene. A square substantial table covered with a white cloth, in the centre a large bowl of roses and honeysuckle; home-made bread and golden butter, a glass dish of honey in its comb, a plate of fresh watercress, and a currant loaf completed the simple fare. Presiding at the tea-tray was a stern, forbidding-looking woman of sixty or more. Opposite her was seated her son, the master of the farm, a heavy-faced, sleepy-looking man and at his side, facing the door, sat Teddy's mother. A sweet, gentle-faced young woman she was, with the same deep, blue eyes as her little son. She bore no resemblance to the older woman, and looked, as she indeed was, superior to her surroundings. Two years ago she had come with her child to make her home amongst her husband's people, and though at first her mother-in-law, Mrs. Platt, was inclined to look upon her contemptuously as a poor, delicate, useless creature, time proved to her that for steady, quiet work no one could eclipse her daughter-in-law. Young Mrs. John, as she was called, was now her right hand, and the dairy work of the farm was given over entirely to her.

"Late again, you young scamp!" was the stern greeting of his grandmother, as Teddy appeared on the scene.

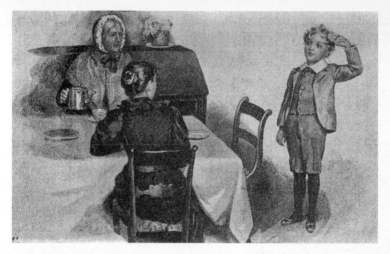

The boy looked at her with a twinkle in his eye, put his little hand to his forehead, and gave her a military salute.

"Sorry," was all he said as he slipped into the chair that was waiting for him.

"What have you been doing, Sonny?" asked the young mother, whose eyes had brightened at the sight of him.

"Telling Father's story," replied Teddy with alacrity.

A shadow came over his mother's face, her lips took a distressed curve, but she said nothing, only occupying herself with attending to the child's wants.

"Your father was never late for his meals," the grandmother put in with asperity.

"Never, Granny? Not when he was a boy? I shall be always on time when I'm a soldier."

"Better begin now, then; bad habits, like weeds, grow apace!"

Teddy had no answer for this; his mouth was full of bread and butter, and he did not speak until the meal was over. Then, while tea was being taken away by the women, he turned to his uncle, who, pulling out a pipe from his pocket, sat down by the open door to smoke.

"Uncle Jake!"

A grunt was the only response; but that was sufficient. The two perfectly understood each other, and a minute after Teddy was perched on his knee.

"I'm wondering if I can have an enemy!" The boy proceeded, folding his small arms and looking up at his uncle steadily. "All good people had enemies in the Bible, and I don't have one. I would like to have a good, down-right enemy!"

"To fight?" asked his uncle.

"To carry on with, you know. He would lay traps for me, and I would for him, like David and Saul. We should have a fine time of it. And then perhaps, if he did something dreadfully wrong, Mother would let me fight him, just once in a while. Don't you think that would be nice?"

"Fighting isn't the only grand thing in this world. Peace is grander," was the slow response to this appeal.

"That's what Mother says. She made me learn this morning, 'Blessed are the peacemakers!' But you must have an enemy to make peace with, and I don't have one."

There was silence. The uncle puffed away at his pipe. He was a good man, and had more brains than his appearance warranted, but Teddy's speeches were often a sore puzzle to him.

The boy continued in a slow, thoughtful tone, "I saw someone today that I feel might be an enemy, but she's a girl. Men don't fight with women."

"I would rather tackle a man than a woman any day. They are powerful enemies sometimes, lad! And what has this young maid done to you?"

"She said,"—and Teddy's eyes grew bright while the blood rushed into his cheeks—"she said she didn't believe a word of Father's story—not a word of it! And she laughed, and walked away."

"That was going it strong. Who is she, to talk so?"

"She's a stranger. Sam said she's come to live with old Sol at the turnpike."

"That must be Grace's child," said old Mrs. Platt, coming and joining in the conversation. "I heard she was coming to stay with her father this summer, and glad I am of it too—the old man is very lonely. I suppose her husband is at sea again."

"What is her husband?" inquired Teddy's mother, as with work in hand she came out and took a seat in the old-fashioned porch.

"A sailor. Grace was always a roving nature herself. She never would settle down quiet and take a husband from these parts. She was maid to our squire's lady then, and went to foreign parts with her, but folks say she's steadied down now wonderful. They've been living at Portsmouth, she and her little girl."

CHAPTER II

WHEN GREEK MEETS GREEK
THEN COMES THE TUG OF WAR

Two determined little figures with flushed, resolute faces, stood opposite one another on a narrow foot-bridge over a running stream.

Neither could pass the other, but neither intended to go back, and the sturdy maiden in her sailor dress, with her small hands placed on her hips, appeared quite a match for Teddy, who, with his golden head well up, looked like a war-horse scenting the battle-field.

It was thus they met again. Both employing their Saturday afternoon in roaming along the edge of a stream, they had suddenly come face to face with one another.

"You must let me come over first," she asserted very emphatically, "because I'm a girl."

"Boys never go back, and a soldier's son never! I'm not going to turn my back before the enemy—I would disgrace my button if I did."

"That old button!" The tone was that of utmost scorn.

Teddy's cheeks grew rosy red at once, but he said nothing.

"I got to this bridge before you did," she continued.

"I began to cross it first. And you... Who are you? No one knows anything about you. I have been crossing this bridge for years."

"More reason you shouldn't cross it now. My name is Nancy Wright—that's who I am." A princess could not have revealed her name more royally. She added, after a pause, "And I mean to come over first, so go back."

"Never! I never go back!"

"Then I shall push you over in the water."

"Come on and try, then!"

Then there was silence; both the little people eyed each other defiantly, yet a little doubtfully, as if measuring one another's strength. Their faces grew eager at the coming contest.

"Boys always ought to give way to girls. Always," Nancy said, using her strongest plea. "You are not a proper boy at all."

"You are not a proper girl. You are wearing a boy's hat and a boy's jacket."

"I'm a sailor's daughter, and everybody can see I am. You say you are a soldier's son, why don't you dress like one?"

Teddy felt he was getting the worst of it. He fingered his button proudly. "I'm wearing something that has been in the thick of a bloody battle; that's more than you can do. Sailors don't know much of fighting."

"They know just as much as soldiers, and as to your old button, I believe you just picked up the old brass thing from the gutter!"

"If you weren't a girl, I would fight you!" sputtered Teddy now, with rising wrath.

"Pooh! I expect I could lick you. I don't believe you have half as big a muscle as I have on my arm."

"A girl have muscle! It's just a bit of fat!"

The tone of scorn proved too much for Nancy's self-control. With a passionate exclamation, she made a quick rush across the plank. There was a struggle, and the result was what might have been expected—a great splash, a scream from Nancy, and both little figures were immersed in the stream. Happily the water was not very deep. After a few minutes scrambling they were on dry ground, considerably sobered by their immersion. Teddy began to laugh a little shamefacedly, but Nancy was very near tears.

"I'll tell my mother you nearly drowned me dead."

"If you are a sailor's daughter, you shouldn't be afraid of the water. Sailors and fish are always in the sea."

"They are never in it, never!"

"Well, they are on it, as close as they can be to it. Why, you are nearly crying! But you are only a girl, and a sailor's girl can't be very brave—not like a soldier's girl would be."

"Sailors are much braver than soldiers," said Nancy, quickly swallowing down her tears; "and when they do fight they are in much more danger than the soldiers. Father said, 'How would soldiers like the earth to swallow them up just when they've been fighting hard and got the victory?' That's what the sea does to the poor sailors. Their ship begins to sink, and they send up three cheers for queen and country, and then stand on deck with folded arms, and go down, down, down to the bottom of the sea, and never make a cry!"

Nancy forgot her wet clothes in her eloquence, and Teddy stared wonderingly at her.

"Well," he said, as if considering the matter, "they may be brave sometimes, but they don't fight like the soldiers. They have no banners, and red coats, and band; and they don't know how to march. A sailor walks any which way. I saw one once, and I thought he was tipsy, but he wasn't. A sailor walks like a goose— he waddles!"

"You are the horridest, rudest boy I've ever seen!"

And with the utmost dignity Nancy walked away, Teddy calling after her, "You made a pretty good charge for a girl, but you couldn't get past me!" And then with one of his loud whoops he raced home, and hardly drew a breath until he reached the farmhouse door. His grandmother confronted him at once.

"You young rascal, what have you been doing? You are never a day out of mischief. If I was your mother I would give you a good whipping; but she spoils you."

"And you do, too, Granny!"

Teddy's laughing blue eyes, as he raised them to the grim face before him, conquered, as they generally did.

"There, go to your mother. She's in the dairy; I wash my hands of you."

But Teddy crept up to his little room to change his wet clothes before he met his mother, and then was very silent about his adventure, merely saying, by way of explanation, that he had fallen into the brook; but at tea, a short time after, he suddenly said, "If you put a sailor and a soldier together, which would you choose, Uncle Jake?"

"Eh, my laddie? Well, they are both good in their way. I couldn't say, I'm sure."

"Mother, wouldn't you say the soldier was the bravest?"

"Perhaps I might, Sonny; but a sailor can be quite as brave."

Teddy's face fell. "I never thought a sailor could fight at all," he said, in a disappointed tone. "I thought they just took care of our ships, and now and then fired a big gun off."

"Who has been bringing up the sailors to you?" asked his grandmother.

"That little girl I told you of—Nancy is her name."

"Where did you see her?"

"Down by the brook; we fell into the water together, because we both wanted to cross at once.

"But, my boy, that was naughty of you not to give place to her," and Mrs. John spoke reprovingly.

"I know it was, Mother, but I was not going to turn back. That would be running away from the enemy. You see, we met in the middle, and she is not at all a nice girl. She is so proud and stuck up about the sailors!"

"As proud as you are of the redcoats, I guess!" old Mrs. Platt said.

"Do sailors and soldiers like each other?" questioned Teddy, ignoring the thrust.

"I am sure I don't know," his mother answered, smiling. "I have never seen them together that I remember, but I should think they did. They both fight for their queen and country."

"Well, I'm a soldier's son, and I don't like a sailor's daughter, I know that! I think she is a kind of enemy."

"Oh, hush, Sonny! You must not have any enemies. It is wrong to talk so."

"That's what he was saying to me the other day," put in his uncle slowly. "He says he wants one."

"Yes, I do," and Teddy gave a fervent nod as he spoke. "And Mother, I believe most good people have enemies. So it must be right to have one."

"They never make one, as you are trying to do."

Teddy looked puzzled.

"Well," he said presently, "I guess it's because she's a stranger. She doesn't belong to our village. I don't like strangers."

"She's no more a stranger than you were when you first came here," his mother said, "and the fact of her being a stranger ought to make you kind to her."

"I'm thinking of calling on her mother," old Mrs. Platt said, looking at her little grandson with her keen gray eyes. "Shall I take you with me to see the little girl?"

"I've seen her enough, Granny. Please, I think I would rather not."

The subject was dropped, but Teddy's thoughts were busy. He ran down to the village green after tea, and there met one or two of his special chums, to whom he confided the events of the afternoon. They highly applauded the scene at the bridge, but Teddy shook his curly head a little doubtfully.

"Men ought always to give way to women, I've heard Mother say. But I couldn't turn back, you see— it would have disgraced my button."

"Tell you what," cried Harry Brown, commonly known as "Carrots" from his fiery hair, "you could have done what the goats did in the primer at school— you ought to have laid flat down and let her walk across you."

"She would have hurt dreadful," Teddy observed thoughtfully. "Besides, she's so proud, I don't think I would have liked to do that."

"No," put in Sam Waters, "you did fine. I say, let's come up to the turnpike and see if she's around there.

I'll give her a word, if she begins to sauce me."

Teddy agreed to this, and the trio trotted off along a flat, dusty road, Teddy beguiling the way by some of his wonderful stories until they came in sight of the low thatched cottage, covered with roses, that guarded the turnpike.

They soon saw the young damsel, for she was swinging on the gate, her dark hair flying in the wind, and her eyes and cheeks bright with the exercise. She looked at the boys, then laughed.

"Poor little button-boy!" she said. "You have to be taken care of by two bigger ones."

"We have come to see you," said Sam valiantly, "because we are not going to stand any cheek from you; so you had better look out."

Nancy stopped swinging, and resting her fat little elbows on the topmost bar, asked saucily, "Did the button-boy tell you to come and help him fight me? Are you all three going to try?"

"We don't fight girls," said Teddy.

"You push them into the water."

"I didn't."

"I told Mother about it. She thought you were a very rude boy not to wait until I crossed over."

There was silence, then Carrots started forward.

"Look here, you'll have to learn your manners. We won't have a strange girl like you stick yourself up so. We have come to tell you to look out for yourself if you don't stop it."

Nancy laughed again, and swung herself violently backward and forward. "Yo ho, my lads! Yo ho!" she sang. "I'm on my ship, and I don't care for boys a bit. They are all as silly as can be. Yo ho! We go! Yo ho, lads, heave ho!"

Her elevated position certainly seemed to give her an advantage.

"We will soon shake you off there!" shouted Sam, his wrath rising at her calm indifference to the lords of creation.

"Come on and try. I'm up the rigging, and a storm is beginning. Hurray—come on!"

Sam and Carrots made a furious onslaught, and the gate was roughly handled, but the more it shook and swung, the more derisive was Nancy's laughter, as she clutched a firm hold with her small hands, and swayed to and fro, calling out excitely, "Furl the main-sail! Stand by, lads—steady—starboard hard! Port your helm! Rocks to leeward! Reef the top-sail! Breakers ahead! Yo ho!"

Teddy looked on, awed by these nautical terms, which seemed to slip so easily from her lips. To him they seemed wonderfully clever, but he was not one to stand aside long in a scene of excitement, and with one of his wild war whoops he rushed forward.

"On, boys! Charge! Hurrah!"

The gate rocked violently, and Nancy began to feel her position was a perilous one. All the little people were screaming at the top of their voices, when suddenly, in the midst of the din, appeared old Sol.

"What now! Who are these trying to break one of Her Majesty's gates down? Be off, you young ruffians! Teddy Platt, you are at the bottom of all the mischief brewing in the parish. I'll get my big stick out and give you a thrashing before I've done with you."

Old Sol's words were fierce, but the boys knew he had the softest heart in the village, and they stood their ground.

"It's all the button-boy," said Nancy eagerly, as she descended from her perch, and laid her little hand confidingly on the old man's arm. "He brought these boys up to fight me, but I was up the mast, and they couldn't shake me off!"

"We told you we would not fight a girl!" protested Teddy indignantly. "You don't speak the truth."

"Well, what did you bring the boys for?" demanded the small maiden severely.

"We came," put in Sam boldly, "to tell you that if you were so cheeky you would soon get into trouble. We aren't going to stand sauce from you."

"What has the little lass been doing, you young scoundrels?"

"They are only boys, Grandfather. Let us go in to Mother, and leave them. They are the rudest boys I've ever seen, and the button-boy is the worst, and his button isn't worth a farthing!"

There was a yell from all three boys at this.

"That's it!" cried Carrots excitedly. "It's the button she's so cheeky about. We aren't going to have Teddy's button laughed at. We won't stand it, Sol—we won't!"

"It shows she doesn't know anything, or she would not talk so. She's just a baby, that's what she is."

"Why, she doesn't believe Father's story is true, Sol! You know it is, don't you?"

"She isn't as old as the button itself."

"Ha! Ha! She wasn't born when it was in battle. Much she knows about it!"

Sol had difficulty in quieting the indignant voices.

"Look here, you boys, go home and leave my little lass to me. She knows nothing about the button. I'll tell her the story, and then she won't laugh at it any more. Ay, I remember seeing your father, youngster. He was a brave man, he was, but he would never have made war against little maids like this. Shame on you. Go home! Go away, I say, or I'll bring my stick out."

"She's been told the story. She listened, and she laughed. She ought to say she is sorry." Teddy stood with his legs wide apart, and his hands in his pockets. His tone was severe.

"I'll never, never, never say I'm sorry. I'm glad of what I said. I don't believe a word of it!"

And with this parting shot Nancy ran into the cottage, and the boys returned to the village more slowly than they came.

"Mother," said Teddy that night, as his mother bent down for a good-night kiss, "I haven't been good today, and I don't feel good now. I feel, when I think it over, so angry inside."

"What is it about, Sonny?"

"Father's button." The tone was drowsy, and seeing his eyelids droop heavily Mrs. John said no more, only breathed a prayer that her little son might fight as bravely for Christ's honour as he did for that of his father's button.

CHAPTER III

A RECRUITING SERGEANT

It was Sunday morning. Along a sweet-scented lane, with shady limes overhead and honeysuckle and wild roses growing in profusion on the hedges at each side, walked Teddy's mother, holding her little son tightly by the hand. The bells of the village church were ringing out for the service, and groups of two and three were passing in at the old lych-gate. Mrs. John was talking in her sweet, clear voice to her boy, and he, letting his restless blue eyes rove to and fro, noting every bird on the hedges and every flower in the path, kept bringing them back to his mother's face with a dreamy upward gaze. "I will try, Mother, I really will. I will keep my hands tight in my pockets, and my feet close together. I will pretend I'm going to be shot by a file of soldiers, and I really think that will help me not to fidget. I promise you that I'll be good today."

And having received this promise from him, Mrs. John passed into church with a relieved mind. Teddy's restless little body was a sore trial to anyone who sat next to him in church, and many were the lectures that had been bestowed on him by Sunday-school teacher and pastor, besides the gentle admonitions of his mother.

As Teddy quietly perched himself on the seat beside his mother, he murmured to himself, "Twenty soldiers in front of me, twenty rifles pointing—I shall stand like a rock —I'll set my teeth, and I shan't even blink my eyes. Now I see the officer coming—he's going to say, 'Present!' I'm not moving a muscle. In five minutes more they will give me . . ."

His active brain here received a check. There on the opposite side, facing him was Nancy, seated between her mother and old Sol. She was still in her sailor suit, and with her dark, mischievous brown eyes fixed steadily on him, Teddy could not remain unmoved beneath her gaze for long. His little hands were working nervously in his coat pockets. Why did she stare at him so? Well, he could stare back, and then blue eyes and brown confronted each other for some moments with unblinking defiance in their gaze. At last Teddy's patience gave way, and twisting up his little features into a most queer grimace, he mounted a hassock to give her the full benefit of it.

Instantly, out came a little red tongue at him, and at this daring piece of audacity he gasped out loud, "I hate you!"

Then, as all eyes in the surrounding pews were turned upon him, and his mother's shocked gaze met his, Teddy crimsoned to the roots of his hair, and taking up a large prayer-book, he used it as a shield from his small antagonist during the remainder of the service. As the congregation was leaving the church later on, the rector made his way to young Mrs. Platt, who was lingering talking to a neighbour. He was a gray-haired, gentle-faced man, with a slow, dreamy manner in speaking.

"Mrs. John, what has happened to make your little boy so forget himself this morning?"

"Indeed, Sir, I cannot say. I really thought he was going to be good today."

"I think he had better come to tea with me this afternoon, and we will have a little talk together."

Teddy looked up with awe in his blue eyes. He well knew that this was the rector's usual practice when any delinquent was brought before his notice, but it had never yet fallen to his lot to receive the invitation. Mr. Upton had his own way of doing things, so people said, and he had greater faith in reasoning with any culprits than scolding them, whether they were grown men or women, or children.

Teddy's restless ways in church had been a trial to him for a long time, and he felt that this morning's action must receive a check.

"Thank you, Sir," responded Mrs. John. "He will come to you after Sunday-school is over this afternoon."

And Teddy, completely sobered, walked home beside his mother without uttering a word.

At half-past four he stood on the rectory doorsteps looking into the cool broad hall in front of him, which led out of a glass door at the opposite end into a brilliant flower garden. Spotless white carpet covered the floor and stairs, and everything indoors denoted a careful housekeeper. Mr. Upton was a widower, and was to a great extent ruled by two or three old and faithful servants.

As the boy stood there, the rector appeared and led him into his study.

"We have half an hour before tea to have a little conversation, my boy. Sit down, and tell me what you have been learning at Sunday-school this afternoon.

"Teacher was telling us about the children of Israel in Egypt. I'm afraid I don't remember very much what he said, for I was busy thinking about coming to see you."

Mr. Upton smiled, and drew the child on to talk. Then, after he was thoroughly at ease, he put a large Bible in front of him.

"I want you to read me a verse in the First Epistle of John, in the third chapter. It is the fifteenth verse; can you find it?"

"Yes, Sir," and with an eager importance Teddy turned over the leaves.

"Whosoever hateth his brother is a murderer," he read solemnly.

"That will do. Now think it over for five minutes in silence, and then tell me what your thoughts are about it."

The boy hung his head in shame; he folded his arms and sat immovable until the five minutes were over, then he said timidly, "I wouldn't hate a brother. I would like to have one. Do you think it means the same when it's a girl?"

"Precisely the same—a brother means any person in the world, man, woman, or child."

"Then I ought to be hung."

There was much self-pity in Teddy's tone. Mr. Upton did not smile, he was gazing abstractedly out of the window, and said slowly, "The root of murder is anger. The same motive that prompts a passionate statement, prompts a passionate and perhaps fatal blow."

There was silence. Then in a more cheerful tone the rector turned to the little culprit.

"And now tell me the whole story, and who it was that you spoke to in church."

Teddy was perfectly ready with his defence, and he poured into his listener's ears such a voluble story that the rector was quite bewildered when it came to an end.

"It's Father's button I care about," added the boy, fingering his beloved object proudly, "and she didn't believe me a bit. She put out her tongue as long as ever she could!"

"Tell me the story of the button. I have heard it, but I have forgotten the details."

Teddy's eyes sparkled, and his little head was raised erect again. Slipping off his chair, he stood in front of the rector, and told the oft-repeated tale with dramatic force and effect. Mr. Upton listened with interest, but before he could offer any comment on it, tea was announced, and taking the child by the hand he marched him into the dining-room.

Hot tea-cakes, strawberry jam, and plum cake kept our little friend fully occupied for some time. He wondered if all the naughty boys interviewed by the rector had been treated to the same fare. He began to think an invitation to Sunday tea at the rectory highly desirable.

"And now," said Mr. Upton, toward the end of the meal, "I want some more talk with you. Your father was a brave soldier. He died in saving the colours. You want to grow up like him, do you not?"

"Yes, Sir. Indeed I do."

"There is a little verse in God's Word that describes our Lord's banner—His colours. Will you say it after me?—'His banner over me was love.'"

Teddy repeated the verse slowly, and with interest. "It is a wonderful banner," pursued Mr. Upton thoughtfully, "The enemy confronted with it on every side. In the thick of the fight we can but hoist our colours: 'Love.' God's love to man, when man is fighting from his infancy against his Maker. What host would march to meet the foe with such a banner, dyed red with the life-blood of their Captain, the Son of God, the Saviour of the world?"

Teddy drew a long breath, and when the rector paused, he cried enthusiastically, "Please go on, Sir. I like to hear it. Will God let me hold up the banner for Him?"

"If you have enlisted in His service, He will. Are you one of His soldiers?"

"I don't know."

"God always wants each of us to present ourselves to Him, if we want to enlist in His army. Have you done that? There must come a time in our lives when we yield ourselves wholly and unreservedly to the One who is our rightful owner. Why, my boy, do you believe that Jesus died on the cross to save you? Did He bear your sins for you there?"

"Yes," said Teddy, fixing his blue eyes earnestly on the rector. "I really believe He did, for Mother has often explained it to me."

"Then how dare you stand aloof from His army? How is it that you have never enlisted? Are you marching along in the enemy's ranks?"

Teddy's small hands were clenched, and his eyes lit up with a great resolve.

"I'll enlist at once, Sir. I'll be one of God's soldiers now."

"How are you going to do it?"

"I don't know. Tell me, please."

There was silence. Mr. Upton met the child's earnest, upward gaze with awe, as he realized how much hung on his words. He had a firm belief that children could by the grace of God lead a consistent Christian life. He knew the Master would accept a child's heart, and guide and keep the frail and helpless steps on the way heavenward. And with a swift prayer for guidance he spoke.

"You must tell God about it yourself, and don't be in a hurry. Kneel down quietly by yourself somewhere, and first of all ask that the Holy Spirit may guide you, that your sins may be blotted out, and your name written in the Book of Life, for the sake of Jesus who died for you. Then tell God you want Him to enlist you, and give yourself right up to Him for now and for all eternity."

Mr. Upton spoke slowly and emphatically; he knew he often preached above the heads of his little hearers, and he strove to speak in simple language now.

Teddy remained very silent; then he said, "And if I enlist, shall I have to be God's soldier for ever and ever, until I'm an old man of a hundred, with white hair and no teeth?"

"Would you rather be one of the devil's soldiers?"

"No."

"You are quite right to think it over. I would rather you did not decide too hastily. Go home and think it over. And come and tell me when you have decided."

The boy's white brow was crumpled with anxious creases.

"I should like to be one of God's soldiers, but who shall I have to fight? Any real enemies, or only make believe?"

"I will tell you about your enemies after you have enlisted. I can show you one very real one that is your worst enemy."

"Can you? A real live one?"

"A real live one."

Teddy smiled contentedly.

"Now," added Mr. Upton, "I am going to send you home. If you enlist, the first person you will have to hold up your banner to is that little girl whom you said you hated. Before you go I want to pray with you. Kneel down with me."

The evening sunshine streamed in through the open window. Alighting on the white hair of the minister and the boy's fair curls, as they knelt together, it bathed them in a golden glory. With closed eyes and folded hands Teddy listened to Mr. Upton's prayer.

"Loving Father, another lamb of Thine I bring to Thee. Guide him in his decision to serve Thee and use him and bless him through all eternity. Grant that he may fight a good fight, and be crowned with glory hereafter. For Jesus Christ's sake. Amen."

An hour later, and Teddy was seated by his mother's side in the old porch. His grandmother and uncle had gone to evening church, and Mrs. John was left with her boy alone.

He had been telling her the substance of his conversation with the rector, and now curled up on the low wooden seat, his small legs crossed underneath him, he was gazing dreamily out into the sweet-scented garden. The bees were droning, and the gnats humming amongst the tall hollyhocks and crimson and white roses close by. The birds were already twittering their last "good-nights" to one another, and a soft, peaceful spell seemed to be falling on all around.

"I feel," he said presently, as he gazed up into the still, blue sky, "as if God is waiting for me, Mother."

Mrs. John did not answer. He added quickly, "When did you enlist, Mother? Long, long ago?"

"Yes, Darling, just before I married your father."

"And when did Father enlist? When he was a little boy like me?"

"Not until he was a grown man, Sonny. He often used to say he wished he had given his heart to God when he was younger."

"I suppose God will take little soldiers? Do you think I shall be the youngest He has?"

"No, Darling. He has many brave little soldiers younger than you."

Another long silence, then a deep-drawn sigh from Teddy.

"I feel I have very big thoughts tonight, Mother. I get so crowded thinking. Will you read to me before I go to bed?"

Mrs. John pressed her lips on the curly head so near her.

"My boy, I am so glad for you to have these thoughts. Mother has often prayed that you may be faithful as one of Christ's little soldiers and servants. Now, what shall I read?"

"Read me about the three men and the burning fiery furnace."

And the young mother took her Bible in hand, and drawing her boy close to her until his little head rested against her shoulder, read him the story he wished.

Later on, as she tucked him up in bed, and was giving him a kiss, he clasped his arms around her neck and whispered, "I think I'm going to do it quite by myself tomorrow."

CHAPTER IV

ENLISTING FOR LIFE

The village children were swarming out of school the next afternoon. The heat and confinement of the crowded schoolroom had not lessened the superabundance of energy and high spirits amongst them. The boys soon congregated on the green, bent on a game of cricket.

"Where's Teddy?"

"Teddy Platt!"

"Young Ted, where has he gone?"

"Fetch Teddy!"

This was the general cry. But Teddy was nowhere to be seen.

"Has he been kept in?" asked one.

"Likely enough. He is up in the clouds today."

"Oh, isn't he just! Why, I offered him half such a huge apple. My! It was a beauty! And his eyes sort of wandered away from it, as if it had been a piece of mud! 'Thanks,' he said, 'I'll have a bite tomorrow— not today.'"

"And Teacher was down on him sharp, too," put in another eager voice. "He answered all the arithmetic wrong, and he said forty soldiers made a rood! And Teacher says, 'Is your head good for nothing but soldiers?' And Ted he got as red as fire, and says, 'It's full of them today, Sir,' and Teacher said, 'Go down to the bottom of the class until you can empty it of them then, and tell me when you have done it.' And when Ted comes next to me I says, 'Is your button lost, old chap, that you are in such a stew?' And he says, 'No, the button is all right, but I'm thinking how to enlist.'"

"He'll go for a drummer-boy as soon as he's big enough, and I'll go with him!" cried Carrots.

"Oh, come on!" shouted one of the impatient ones. "If Ted's not here, let us begin without him."

And Teddy's delinquencies at school were soon forgotten in the excitement of the game.

He had not been kept in, but had slipped away the minute school was over, and was soon dodging in and out of the thick, overhanging trees along the edge of his favourite stream. His little feet sped swiftly along, and as he ran he talked in a whisper to himself, which was his way when anything special was weighing on his mind. "I'll go right into the wood, and get under a thick tree. I won't let a squirrel see me, nor even a rabbit. I must be quite quiet. It must be like church, and I won't come away until I've done it."

Into the wood he went, but he was hard to satisfy; roaming here and there, peeping around corners, and thrusting his curly head in amongst the bushes, it was fully half an hour before he chose his spot.

It was a secluded little nook under an old oak-tree, where the moss grew thick and green, and bushes of all sorts and sizes formed a natural bower around the marred trunk. In front of this tree Teddy stood, and then, half shyly, half reverently, he took off his cap and laid it on the ground. Looking up through the veil of green leaves above him to the sunny blue sky beyond, he stood with clasped hands and parted lips for a moment or two in perfect silence. The soft wind played gently with his curls, and rustled amongst the leafy boughs overhead, and in the distance the birds' sweet voices were the only sounds that met his ears. As the boy's eyes came back to earth they seemed to have reflected in them something of the bright sunshine above, and then down on his knees he dropped.

Placing his little clasped hands against the old trunk in front of him, and bending his golden head until it rested likewise against the tree, Teddy prayed aloud, slowly, and with frequent pauses, "O God! Here I am. Have You been waiting for me? I've come to enlist. And, please, I forget all Mr. Upton told me to say. But will You forgive me my sins, and write my name down in Your book in heaven? —Edward James Platt is my name. I've come to be Your soldier for ever and ever. Will You please keep me always? I never want to go back from being Your soldier. Make me fight a grand fight, and help me to hold Your colours up well. And please, God, will You tell Father I've enlisted this afternoon? Mr. Upton said You would take me. I thank You for letting Jesus die for me, and I'm very sorry I haven't belonged to His army before, but I didn't quite understand that He wanted me. Help me to be a good boy, for Jesus Christ's sake. Amen."

A child's prayer, but it was prayed with a child's strong faith. As Teddy rose to his feet, he had the assurance that God had accepted him. That scene in the wood, when he dedicated himself to the service of the King of kings, would be stamped on his memory as long as he lived. And now that the deed was done a great load seemed to be lifted off his mind. He came into the midst of the boys on the green a short time afterward with a radiant face, and took his share in fielding, bowling, and batting with such a vigour and will, that he proved himself the hero of the hour. Later in the evening he wandered into the dairy, where his mother was busy, and asked her if he could go and see the rector.

"What for, Sonny?"

"He asked me to come. Is it too late, do you think? I should like to go tonight."

Mrs. John looked down upon the eager little face lifted to hers.

"Run away, then, but don't stay long."

And so it was that for the second time that week Teddy was a visitor at the rectory.

"Please, Sir, I've done it!" he exclaimed breathlessly, as soon as he was ushered into the presence of the rector.

"Eh? What have you been doing?"

And Mr. Upton roused himself from a reverie into which he had fallen as he sat at his study window and watched his favourite beehives. Then, noting the disappointed look on the child's face, and recognizing who it was, he added briskly, "Ah! It is Teddy Platt, is it? And so you have done it, have you? Thank God! Yes, I remember all about it. You are a fresh recruit."

Teddy's eyes glistened. "I enlisted this afternoon, Sir."

"For life, did you? No short service system with God!"

Mr. Upton had at one time been chaplain to troops abroad, and it was his knowledge of military matters that so attracted the boy.

"Yes, for life, Sir."

"May God keep you true to Him, my boy, in life and in death!"

There was a pause, then Teddy said eagerly, "Please, Sir, you said you would show me one of the enemies I have got to fight."

"Ah! Did I? One of the many—which one, I wonder?"

"'A real live one,' you said."

"Yes, I remember. Come this way."

He led the child into his drawing-room in front of a large mirror reaching down to the ground, and told him to find his enemy there.

"Why, it's only myself!" Teddy said in a disappointed tone, though there was wonder in his eyes.

"That's it—yourself—small Teddy Platt is your worst enemy. The older you live the more you will discover what a very formidable and mighty enemy he is."

"Please, Sir, I don't understand."

"Sit down here, by me, and let me try to explain it to you. If you are going to try to serve the Lord Jesus Christ, you will find that you will have two Teddies to deal with—a good one and a bad one. The bad one is your enemy. Now, you told me you were angry with that little girl. Are you angry still?"

"I've forgotten all about her. I—I don't love her."

"The bad Teddy in you doesn't like her, but the good Teddy will. Now you must fight against the bad Teddy, and overcome him. Jesus will help you. You can't fight without Him."

"I think I know," said Teddy thoughtfully. "Last week some fellow said, 'Come and get some apples from the Park orchard.' I wanted to dreadful. That was my bad self, but I thought it would be stealing, and I didn't go. That was my good self, wasn't it?"

"Quite right! Keep close to your Captain. Our Officer always leads, and remember—'Forward! No quarter to the enemy!'"

Then gazing abstractedly out into the garden, Mr. Upton added, as if to himself, "'But I see another law in my members, warring against the law of my mind, and bringing me into captivity to the law of sin, which is in my members . . . Who shall deliver me from the body of this death? I thank God through Jesus Christ our Lord. So then with the mind I myself serve the law of God, but with the flesh the law of sin.'"

The next day, when at dinner, for it was generally at meal times Teddy chose to make his observations, he looked around the table appealingly.

"What's the very ugliest name that could be given a boy?"

"Sakes alive?" ejaculated his grandmother. "And who may you be wanting to christen?"

"It isn't for a baby; a boy about as old as me. What do you think is an ugly name?"

"I don't think any name is very ugly," his mother said. "If you like a person, their name always seems to fit. I knew two boys named Tobiah and Eli. I didn't like the names at first, though they are Bible ones. But when I got to know and like the boys, I also liked the names."

"I want a much more hideous name," asserted Teddy. "Some name that would describe a very wicked person."

"I hope you are not going to call anyone by it," observed his grandmother suspiciously.

Teddy lifted his blue eyes up to her solemnly. "I expect I'll find one for myself," he said. And nothing more could be got out of him.

After dinner, a half-holiday having been given the school children, Teddy stole out to the woods. When out of sight he began a brisk conversation with himself, as was his custom. It may give us an insight into his busy brain if we listen.

"Goggles might do, or Grubby, or Toad. I want to have some name, else I won't be able to talk to him so well. I wish Mother had helped me. It's very difficult. I can't seem to think of a name quite ugly enough. I expect perhaps Mr. Upton could tell me. I'll wait and ask him. I hope I won't have to wait long, for I want it all settled, so that I can begin to fight properly with him. Now I've got to find Nancy. Mr. Upton said I was to be friends with her. I've got to hold up my banner of love over her. I hope she'll like it. She's a horrid—stop, that's my enemy just going to speak! A horrid girl, you were going to say, were you? Now you just get out. Nancy is a very nice girl—at least, she soon will be. I'll try and think her nice, I will. I've got to fight you, enemy, if you say such things. Why, I do declare, there she is climbing that tree!"

Teddy's conversation came to an end, and he stared with open mouth and eyes at the nimble way Nancy was climbing up an old beech-tree. He gave a shrill whistle, which made the little girl look around. Not a bit disconcerted was she.

"Aha, it's the silly little button-boy. You can't catch me!"

It was a challenge. Instantly Teddy stripped off his jacket, and darted to the tree. She had a good start. Even he caught his breath in wonder at her rapid ascent, and the fearless way in which she seemed to plant her small feet on the most fragile-looking branches. Up they went, panting with the exercise, but at length she could go no further, and seating herself on a comfortable bough she looked mischievously down at him.

"You couldn't catch me. You don't know how to climb! My father taught me. I can go up the rigging as far as any sailor boy, and this is my ship, but I'll let you sit down by me if you behave yourself."

Teddy swung himself across a bough opposite her, and was silent for a moment. Each child was trying to recover its breath, and Teddy was considering how to make peace. He did it in his own quaint fashion.

"I think we're pretty close to heaven," he remarked presently, lifting his soft blue eyes to the clear sky above. "I wonder if that's the reason birds in their nests agree? The angels can't like to hear quallering so close to them."

"I'm not going to quarrel, and you didn't say that word right."

"What word?"

"Quarrering." And Nancy's tone was emphatic, though a doubt stole into her own mind as to whether her pronunciation was correct. But Teddy was too intent on pulling something out of his pocket to notice her correction. He slowly unrolled a large white pocket-handkerchief, tied it carefully to a twig, which he broke off from an adjoining branch, and then held it up in front of her.

"I did it myself this morning," he said with pride. "I asked Uncle Jake for one of his best handkerchiefs. He gave it to me last night, and I did it with a pen and ink before breakfast. Can you read it?"

Nancy looked at the straggling, uneven black letters that occupied the whole width across.

"Love?" she said curiously; "what does that mean?"

"It's my banner of love that I'm going to carry for my Captain. It means I've got to love even you."

Nancy's red lips pouted. "I don't want you to love me," she said.

"I've got to do it."

"How are you going to do it?"

"I'm—I'm not quite sure. I'm never going to be angry with you. And it's very hard . . ." Here a deep-drawn sigh broke from him. "It's very hard, but I've got to tell you I'm sorry I wouldn't let you cross the bridge first. I'm sorry I said I hated you in church."

Nancy's bright, dark eyes peered inquisitively into the dreamy, blue ones opposite her.

"Are you really sorry?" she said.

"I think I am, at least part of me is. My enemy isn't, but I am."

This was beyond Nancy's comprehension.

"And you'll never get angry, or set those horrid boys at me any more?"

"No. I never will."

Here a big rosy-cheeked apple was produced hastily out of the other pocket, and presented as a peace offering.

It was taken in silence. Then as Nancy's white little teeth met in it she said, with one of her beaming smiles, "And do I have to love you?"

"I think you had better, because it will make it easier."

"Well, I will then, if you'll do one thing."

"What is it?"

"Give me that old button of yours."

Teddy fairly gasped at this audacity.

"Give you Father's button!" he cried. "Never, never, never! I would rather be shot dead, or drowned dead, or hung dead, or chopped into little tiny bits! I'll never give it up! It's going to be on my coats and waist-coats until I'm a hundred, and then it will be buried in my grave with me. Suppose I lost my button, do you know what I would do?"

Nancy gazed at the young orator with a little awe.

"No," she said. "What?"

"I would drop down and die. My heart would burst and break. If I couldn't die very quick, I wouldn't eat or drink nothing. I'd go sadly to my grave and lay my head down. The next morning you would find me stiff and cold with my glassy eyes staring up at the sky, like an old dog I read about."

Teddy's tone was so intensely tragic that Nancy was silent. At last she said, "I'll never love you proper until you give it to me."

"Will you like me a little instead?"

"I might do that," she replied reluctantly.

"And you won't never say you don't believe Father's story?"

"I'm not going to promise."

Then, as the very last bite was taken of the apple, she added, "I'll hear some more of your stories first. I want to hear one now. Sally White told me at school you know all about fairies."

Teddy nodded impressively, then said slowly, "I make believe I do. But I don't make- believe Father's story."

"Tell me a story now."

Teddy clasped his hands around a bough, and with knitted brows considered. Then he looked up, and the light sparkled in his eyes.

"Shall I tell you about when I went into an oak tree, and found a little door leading down some steps that took me to the goblin's cave?"

This sounded enchanting, and Nancy eagerly prepared herself to listen. Such a story was then poured out that it held her spell-bound. Goblins, elves, and fairies, underground glories, thrilling adventures and escapes. Was it any wonder that with such a gift for story-telling Teddy was the king of the village? It came to an end at last. Nancy drew a long breath of relief and content when she heard the concluding sentence, "And I quickly opened the little door, and there I was outside the oak. Safe in the wood again."

"Button-boy, I do like you," she asserted, with a quick little nod of her head. "Will you tell me another story soon?"

"Perhaps I will," said Teddy, feeling a little elated that he was gaining supremacy over her. "But I'm going home now. I only came out to have a think, and to make friends with you."

"What made you come and make it up?" the little maiden asked, as after a scramble down, they stood at the foot of the tree. "You said something about your Captain; who is He?"

"Jesus Christ," Teddy replied reverently, "and His banner is love, so I have to love everybody, whether I like them or not."

"Why?"

"Because He wants me to. I'm one of His soldiers now."

"Does Jesus have any sailors?"

The question was put suddenly, and the answer was given with a slight air of superiority, "No, He has only soldiers."

"Then I don't want to belong to Him. I believe He has sailors just as well as soldiers, only you're not telling true."

Her tone was getting wrathful, but Teddy shook his head solemnly. "I'm sure there's nothing about Jesus' sailors in the Bible. But I'll ask Mother, and then I'll tell you. I must go home now. Good-bye. We're going to be friends?"

"Yes, we're going to be friends," she repeated; and then away they scampered in different directions, Nancy calling out, like a true little woman, "But I shan't really love you till you give me your button."

CHAPTER V

FIRST VICTORIES

"Please, Sir, may I speak to you?" Mr. Upton was coming out of church after a choir practice, when Teddy confronted him.

He smiled when he saw the boy. "You may walk with me and speak to me as much as you like."

And so they sauntered up the shady lane: the old rector with his head bent and his hands crossed behind him, and the boy all eager excitement and motion, with suppressed importance in his tone.

"I want you to give me a name for my enemy, please, Sir."

Mr. Upton looked amused. "Have you had any battles with him yet?"

"I think I had one yesterday. May I tell you? Granny was very angry with me because I had made Uncle Jake's best handkerchief into a banner of love. I didn't really think it was naughty. I wrote 'Love' in ink right across it. I took such pains, for I wanted to show it to Nancy. And when I got home Granny was so angry that she took me by the collar. She locked me into the back kitchen. Mother was out, and I cried. I was so miserable.

Granny said I would come to the workhouse. She called me the wickedest, mischievousest boy she had ever seen, and said she would like to give me a good whipping. And at last I got tired of being miserable. I looked about, and I saw the window was partly open. So I climbed up, and then I thought I would jump out and run away across the fields until Mother came home. I was very happy then. I jumped right out, and then I remembered, but I didn't want to go back again."

"And then the fight began?" suggested the rector, as the boy paused.

Teddy nodded. "I asked God to drive my enemy away, but I was an awful long time thinking it out. Is thinking fighting?"

"Very often it is."

"I did fight hard, then. I climbed in again. Was that being a soldier?"

"Yes, my boy."

"And Granny let me out soon after. I kissed her and said I was sorry. I told her how nearly I had run away, and asked her to see that the window was locked next time, so that I shouldn't have to fight so hard."

"You will have plenty of fighting. Don't shirk the hottest part of the field. That isn't being brave."

"Will you give me a horrid, ugly name, please, Sir?"

"I thought your enemy's name was Teddy."

"No, that's mine; I must have a name for him—a different one, you know."

"How do you like Ego or Ipse?"

"What funny names! I think I like Ipse best. I'll call him Ipse. Shall I?"

But Mr. Upton's thoughts were far away by this time, and presently he said, as if to himself, "'The last enemy that shall be destroyed is death.' 'Nay, in all these things we are more than conquerors, through Him that loved us.' It is a fight with certain victory ahead. Then why do we fail?"

"Shall I fail?" questioned a soft voice by his side.

"'Without Me you can do nothing.' That's our Captain's word. If you fight without Him, you are done for."

"I think I shall sometimes let Ipse have his way. Will that be deserting to the enemy?"

"It will be sure and certain defeat."

"But then, of course, my Captain won't let me be beaten, if I stick close to Him."

And so they talked, a strange couple. But the younger of them had a faith which the elder might envy, and a grasp of the unseen that the ripest saint could not surpass.

Not long after this, Teddy and his schoolfellows were having a delightful afternoon in the woods. It was Saturday afternoon, and they were playing their favourite war game, Teddy, of course, being prime instigator of the whole affair. A few of the more adventurous girls had joined them, Nancy amongst them. Her

respect for Teddy was gradually increasing, though
nothing seemed to quench her self-assertion and inde-
pendence of thought and action. At length Teddy
announced his intention of going off on an expedition
as a scout, and when Nancy insisted that she would
come too. The two children started, making their way
out of the wood and down to the banks of the stream,
which soon joined the river.

"What have we to do?" asked Nancy.

"It's great fun. You see, every one we meet is an
enemy. We have to get past them without them seeing
us. We must crawl through the long grass, or we must
climb a tree, or get through the bushes. We will have all
kinds of adventures."

"And if we don't meet anybody?"

"That's why I came down this way. There are
always a lot of people fishing in the river. Now look
out, don't you talk loud. And step softly. Just think that
the first person who sees us will shoot us dead."

"But they won't."

"You must make believe they will."

Teddy's tone was stern, and Nancy was too occupied in holding her hat on her head as they crept
through some low bushes to advance any more scep-
tical opinions.

And then suddenly, a short time after, they came on
a fisherman. It was only a burly farmer, who was
evidently making a day of it, for he sat under the shade

of a tree with the remnants of a substantial lunch around him. His fishing-rod was in his hand, but the line was out of the water, and he, with head thrown back and mouth wide open, was fast asleep.

"Hush!" said Teddy, in an excited whisper. "If he wakes, all is up with us. Now let's get past him on tiptoe."

This was accomplished safely; but having passed him Teddy stood still, and the spirit of mischief seized hold of him. Turning to Nancy, he said, with sparkling eyes, "What fun it would be to take him prisoner and tie him up to the tree with his own fishing-line! He's an enemy. I really think it's our duty to do it. You stay here and watch me."

Deftly and quickly Teddy set to work, but when he had once passed the line around the farmer's body and the tree, he had no difficulty in finishing the work he had begun. Dancing like an elf with the line in his hand, he spun around and around the tree until the line was wound around to its very last extremity, and the farmer looked like some big bluebottle fly entangled in the fine meshes of a spider's web. Still he slept on, and with a delighted chuckle Teddy sped back to his little companion. Her eyes were dancing with mirth, and she clapped her hands at the successful exploit.

"He'll wake up and won't be able to get away. What fun! How I would like to see him!"

"Come on quick. He's Farmer Green. He's an awful angry man. He gave Sam such a thrashing for tying an old saucepan to one of his pigs' tails. He won't know who has done it. I did tie the knots awful tight."

Away they ran; but they had not proceeded far before Teddy came to a standstill, and all the saucy sparkle died out of his eyes.

"What's the matter?" asked Nancy. "Have you got a pain?"

"I'm afraid I am going to have a fight with Ipse."

The words were uttered almost in a whisper, and Nancy looked on with wonder.

"It isn't right," he said, after a long pause. "I do want—at least, Ipse wants—to leave him there awfully, but Mother would say it was very naughty. I think—I think my Captain doesn't like it. I shall have to go back and undo him."

"Oh, you can't!" cried Nancy. "You'll wake him up. Then you will catch it! Let him undo himself!"

Teddy shook his head, and then stole softly back to the tree, Nancy following him at a respectful distance.

It seemed a harder business to untie the knots than to tie them, but at length it was done, and the unwinding process began. Alas! Farmer Green's nap was over, and with a hasty start, he was roused to the full use of his faculties. When he discovered his condition he got angry and turned on Teddy in great wrath, as he vainly tried to extricate himself.

"Please, Sir," said Teddy, nothing daunted, "if you keep still, I shall undo you very soon. I won't break your line if I can help it."

"You young scoundrel! How dare you show your face, after such an audacious piece of impudence! You are the plague of the parish. A good thrashing is what you will get, sure as my name is Jonathan Green!"

Teddy's face was hot and red, and the spectacle of him trying to unwind the line from the struggling and exasperated farmer was so irresistibly comic to Nancy that she burst out laughing.

Jonathan Green was soon on his feet again. Seizing hold of Teddy by the collar, he shook him like a terrier would shake a rat. Then, without letting go of him, he pulled out a piece of cord from his coat pocket.

"Now, I'll teach you a lesson, Youngster, that you won't forget. It's a good thing I've got this bit of rope."

And in another few minutes he had bound the boy securely to the tree, tying his hands together with his handkerchief. Then, as Nancy stepped forward, indignant at this severe treatment, he turned on her.

"There are two of you, are there? Well, you shall share the same fate till I think fit to release you. I'll teach you to stop playing such impish tricks on decent folk."

"You're the wickedest man that's living, I'm sure!" cried Nancy wrathfully. "Why, he was undoing you when you woke up, which was very kind of him. I wish he had left you tied up, I do!"

But Farmer Green, with a grim smile of satisfaction, soon settled her in the same fashion as he had done the boy. Then, picking up his fishing basket, strode away, calling out, "You'll stay there my time, you young limbs of mischief! It's only serving like you serve!"

"Button-boy, did he hurt you?" asked Nancy anxiously. For all this time Teddy had not said a word.

He turned his head and looked at her. "I feel shooken up dreadful; he's so awful strong; but I'm not very hurt. Only I'm sorry. I've been telling my Captain about it, and asking Him to forgive me."

"Shall we stay here all the evening and all the night?"

"Oh, no! He'll come and let us go soon. It isn't fair for you, for you didn't do anything."

"I laughed at him. I wanted you to leave him tied up. But I don't care. It doesn't hurt. You haven't told me ever what I asked you about Jesus' sailors. Tell me now, because I want to belong to your Captain, and I'm not going to be a soldier."

"I did ask Mother. She said sailors were soldiers. They were sea soldiers. You'll have to be a soldier, I guess."

"Sailors fight, I know they do. Grandfather read me about Nelson the other evening. He showed me a picture of sailors cutting the enemy's arms off, as they tried to scramble on board ship. I shan't never change to soldiers. Sailors are much nicer. And if sailors fight, I can be a sailor for Jesus."

Their conversation was interrupted by voices and steps approaching. In another moment two ladies and a gentleman appeared, evidently going home after a fishing excursion. The path led past the tree. They stopped in astonishment at the sight of the two children.

Teddy was the first to speak. He recognized the newcomers to be the squire, Colonel Graham, and his wife, with a visitor staying with them.

"Please, Sir, will you undo us?" he asked appealingly.

The colonel laughed heartily. "Ah, young fellow, you are caught, are you? Lady Helen, this is one of the young hopefuls in our village. I have been told he is the ringleader in every bit of mischief set going! You wouldn't think it to look at him, would you?"

"What an angel's face!" said that lady admiringly. "And who is the little girl? She looks a regular little gipsy!"

Neither of the children appreciated these remarks, but the colonel good-naturedly put down his fishing basket and cut the piece of rope that bound them.

"Now, then, Youngster," he said, "speak up and tell us who bound you in this fashion! What have you been doing to merit such punishment?"

Having got his hands free, Teddy stood up bravely and told the story briefly and clearly, to the great amusement of his hearers.

"And he would never have been caught if he hadn't gone back to undo him," put in Nancy. "So he shouldn't have been punished at all."

"What made you go back, my boy?" asked Mrs. Graham gently.

The colour rose in Teddy's cheeks. But he never hesitated to speak the truth.

"I went back when I remembered it was wrong to have done it," he said simply.

"But you are not such a paragon of goodness generally," said the colonel. "Wasn't it you and some others who scared our dairymaid into fits one night last winter, by playing pranks after dark, outside the dairy window?"

"Yes, Sir," said Teddy humbly.

"And why didn't you run away when the old man woke?" asked Lady Helen.

"I never run away from anybody," said Teddy, his head more erect than ever. "I'm a soldier's son."

"Capital, my boy. So your father is a soldier? What regiment?"

"He's dead, Sir. May I tell you Father's story?"

"Oh! Ah! I remember now, though I'm not sure that I recollect the details," said the colonel musingly. "Your father was John Platt, who enlisted in one of the line regiments—the 24th, wasn't it? Tell us the story by all means."

Teddy obeyed delightedly, not seeing in the interest of his tale how keenly he was being watched by the ladies. He told it as he always did, with enthusiastic effect. When he offered to show the ladies his button they were charmed with him. The colonel patted him on his head as he left, saying, "Keep your father's spirit in you, my lad, and you'll live to do something great yet!"

"I should like to have him as a page-boy," said Lady Helen, as they walked away. "What a sensitive, refined little face it is!"

"Too good to be spoiled by house service," said Colonel Graham. "His mother is a superior young woman, with a very good education. The Platts are highly respected around here."

The children ran back to their playfellows considerably sobered by their experience. Teddy very soon made his way home, and told his mother all that had befallen him.

"It's dreadfully difficult to remember in time, Mother. I'm not a very good soldier, am I? Do you think I ought to love old Farmer Green? If you won't tell any one, I've been having a talk with Ipse—he's my enemy Mr. Upton told me about—and he—he hates Farmer Green. But I tell him the banner is 'Love,' and we must try to love him. How can I show him I love him, Mother?"

"I think you must wait a little, Sonny. Don't do anything just yet, but try and not have angry thoughts about him. You know it was very naughty of you to act so. I am not a bit surprised that he lost his temper over it."

"I'll never tie up anybody again, Mother. Never!"

CHAPTER VI

THE REDCOATS

M other, Grandmother, some soldiers are coming here!" Teddy tore into the house one morning after school with this announcement. His face was radiant with delight. His mother was laying the cloth for dinner. Old Mrs. Platt was busy dishing up some potatoes.

"Who told you?" asked the latter.

"I saw one—a real live soldier, a corporal with two gold stripes on his red coat, and such white gloves. I went up to him and talked to him."

"Certainly, modesty is lacking with you," observed Mrs. Platt drily.

"Shyness is," said Mrs. John rather quickly, "but he doesn't show forwardness as a rule."

"Sam and Carrots and lots of the boys were with me, Mother. He told us that he and one or two more had come on to get billets—that's the word—billets for the regiment that was marching through on their way to Wales. We shall see them come marching through the village in a few days. He said most of them were going to be put up in the town, but twenty were coming to the Hare and Hounds. They are going to sleep there. He's such a nice man, Mother. He's only going to sleep here tonight. Then he's going on tomorrow to get some more billets ready in the next town he comes to. Couldn't he come to tea this afternoon? Do let me ask him, Granny!"

Mrs. Platt laughed not ill-humouredly. "You would have us take in any scoundrel, provided he wore a red coat, wouldn't you?"

"Soldiers are never scoundrels!" asserted Teddy with hot indignation.

"Do you know all the soldiers in the British Army, then?" said his grandmother.

"I daresay he wouldn't care to come to tea with strangers, Sonny," put in Mrs. John gently.

"I'm sure he would, for he doesn't like the Hare and Hounds. He said he was a teetotaler. That means he doesn't drink any beer. That is what he said."

"Come, that sounds good," Mrs. Platt remarked. "Well, you can ask him in for your father's sake."

Not much dinner could Teddy eat that day. His lessons at school had never seemed so irksome to him. They were over at last. He tore off in search of his new friend, finding him at length sitting under an old yew tree just outside the churchyard.

"Granny says will you come to tea with us?" he asked breathlessly, as he came up to him.

The corporal looked up. He was a fine-looking young man with a frank, bright face. He was reading a well-worn Bible, which he put carefully in his pocket before he rose to his feet.

"That's very kind of your granny," he said, "and I'll come with pleasure. I'm out of it at the Hare and Hounds."

Teddy's quick eyes had spied the Bible.

"Do you like the Bible?" he asked gravely.

"It's my order book," the corporal said with a smile, "and my best friend in the world."

"What's an order book?"

"It gives you your daily commands—just what you are to do and where you are to go. My Captain writes my orders down in His Word for me."

"He's my Captain too," said Teddy with glistening eyes. "You mean the Lord Jesus, don't you? I've enlisted in His army. I'm one of His soldiers."

"Shake hands, little brother, then. We're comrades after all."

"Are all soldiers in Jesus Christ's army?" asked Teddy as they walked away together.

The corporal shook his head sadly. "Hardly any of them in my regiment," he said. "We are nearly seven hundred strong. Only six men besides myself, as far as I can tell, belong to the Lord. A year ago I was an awful blackguard myself. I drank dreadfully, and couldn't give up the drink. But that's all a thing of the past. Since I have belonged to the Lord, He keeps me from it, and many other bad habits. I'll own I fairly dreaded coming to this bit of duty. The sight and smell of the beer is very strong to a man who has been such a slave to it. I must be quartered in public-houses along the whole way."

"You'll have to fight like Mr. Upton told me to, won't you?" said Teddy. "But if our Captain is with us, Mr. Upton says, we won't be beaten."

"No," said the corporal, a light coming into his eyes. "We shall be more than conquerors."

Then, after a pause, he said, "It's very considerate of your granny to ask me to tea. I was just wishing that something could be done in this village for the men coming after me, like we had last year when we marched through the country for the manoeuvres. They gave us a free tea at several of the places we went through. It kept so many from drinking. There's a man coming along here who I'm terribly anxious about. He has been an awful drunkard, and is quite an old soldier. Last New Year's Day he signed the pledge, and he has kept it ever since. He is just on the point of being converted, I hope. We have had many talks together, but if he's billeted in the Hare and Hounds, or any other public-house, for that matter, I don't know what he'll do. There's nothing for them when they come in tired but to sit in the bar or tap-room and drink. They can't get away from it."

Teddy's brow was knitted with deep thought.

"I didn't know soldiers drank too much," he said. "I thought they never did anything wrong."

The corporal smiled. "Not many are of your opinion," he said. "Most folks put us down as a bad lot."

That evening remained in his memory for long after: the sweet-scented garden, and the long, low kitchen, with the happy family party gathered around the table; the clumsy efforts of the reticent farmer to make his guest feel at home; the short, pithy remarks made by Mrs. Platt, and the gentle, soft-voiced young mother, with the golden-haired boy, continually asking quaint questions about a soldier's life—all this came back to him with a keen sense of pleasure in after years. He was only a young fellow after all, and was touched and gratified by the kindness shown to him, for it made him think of his own mother in her village home. When he took his leave he could hardly express his thanks.

Teddy had been allowed to sit up beyond his usual bedtime, and as he put his little hand into the big brown one of the young soldier he said, "Do you mind telling me your name, Corporal?"

"Walter Saxby," was the ready response.

"And what's the name of the poor old soldier who signed the pledge on New Year's Day?"

"Tim Stokes. He's called Bouncer by most of us."

"I shall remember," said Teddy; then turning to his mother and grandmother after Corporal Saxby had disappeared, he said solemnly, "May I bring Bouncer to tea, if I find him? Corporal told me he hadn't properly enlisted as a soldier of the Lord Jesus, but he wants to. Do you think Mr. Upton could get him to enlist while he's here? Or could you, Granny? Perhaps he'd do it for you."

"I don't know what that boy will come to," said Mrs. Platt later on, when Teddy was safe in bed. "Seems to me he has more the making of a minister in him than a soldier. I don't hold with children being too religious. It's forced and unnatural."

"He isn't too good to live," put in Jake slowly, "no youngster can beat him in play."

"I often wonder," Mrs. John said thoughtfully, "whether he will be a soldier after all. He is almost too sensitive to lead the hard, rough life so many do. I doubt he could stand it."

"He's not wanting in pluck and manliness," Mrs. Platt observed, for she always had a good word to say for her little grandson when he was not present. "I found him this morning careering round the field on that fresh young foal, without any saddle or bridle! I gave him a sharp scolding, for it was kicking up its hind legs like mad. He only looked up in my face and laughed. 'It's my charger, Granny,' he says, 'and he smells the battlefield; that's why he's so excited!' I'm sorry these soldiers are going to fill the place. He thinks and talks quite enough of them as it is. We won't have a moment's peace now until they are gone."

Teddy was up very early the next morning to see his friend go off. He had another long conversation with him before wishing him good-bye. Then, with thoughtful face, he went to school, contemplating many plans in his active little brain, and making innumerable mistakes in his lessons in consequence. At twelve o'clock, when free at last, he made his way to the rectory and asked for Mr. Upton, who greeted him very kindly.

"Any more troubles to tell me?"

"No, Sir. But I want to tell you about the soldiers who are coming."

"I have heard about them. It will be a grand time for you, won't it?"

"Please, Sir, could you have a tea-party for them?"

Mr. Upton pushed up his glasses and looked very bewildered.

"A tea-party, did you say?"

"Yes. The corporal said a clergyman gave one hundred soldiers tea in a schoolroom last year, and spoke to them after. The corporal said it would keep them from drinking in the public-houses. He came to tea with us last night, but Granny won't have a lot of them. So I told him I would tell you about it."

"It's rather an undertaking," said Mr. Upton musingly, "but we could do something for them. When are they to be here?"

"In two or three days, the corporal said."

"I think I might manage it. I will go and see Colonel Graham, and find out if he will help."

"I knew you would be able to do it," said Teddy, beaming all over. "And perhaps, Sir, you could tell some of them how to enlist, like you did me. The corporal said I ought to try to be a recruiting sergeant for my Captain, but they wouldn't listen to me, I am sure. I'm going to try to enlist Nancy. I haven't tried half hard enough. But she says she'll only be a sailor for Jesus, not a soldier. Can she be that, Sir?"

Mr. Upton smiled. "Yes, I think she can. Sailors have to keep watch, and learn their drill, and take orders, and fight under their captain, just like soldiers."

And then Teddy went home and electrified his mother by telling her, with an air of great importance, "Mr. Upton and I are going to give the soldiers a tea-party when they come."

The days passed. Mr. Upton was as good as his word. A large tea was provided in the village school-room, Colonel and Mrs. Graham taking a hearty interest in it. When the soldiers came in one hot, dusty afternoon, everything was ready for them.

Teddy and others of the village children crowded around the Hare and Hounds when they arrived. Nancy was foremost of the crowd.

"I don't think much of soldiers," she said, her nose tilted up in disdain. "They are very dirty men, and covered with dust. They've no band, nor flags flying, nor nothing."

If Teddy was disappointed in the look of his heroes, he did not say so, but Sam remarked, "I guess they have left the band and the flags in the town. These are only the ones they can't put up there."

Later in the afternoon Teddy made his way to the old elm outside the Hare and Hounds. Several of the men were resting on the wooden benches, some with pots of beer, and around whom some of the admiring villagers had made a little circle.

He pushed his way in with his accustomed fearlessness.

"Please, is Mr. Tim Stokes here?"

The soldiers laughed, and bandied a few jokes on the comrade alluded to.

"What do you want with him, Youngster?"

"I want to speak to him."

"I guess you'll find him under one of the tables in the tap-room. Old Bouncer is pretty dry after a march like we have had today."

There was a roar of laughter at this, but Teddy did not understand the joke.

"I must not go inside the Hare and Hounds," he said. "I promised Mother I never would. Will you fetch him out for me?"

And turning to a good-natured-looking young fellow, Teddy put his hand coaxingly on his arm. The soldier looked into the boy's fair face with a laugh and

then a sigh, and rising to his feet said, "All right, little chap, I'll fetch him out to you."

He was gone some time. Teddy improved his opportunity by making friends with those around him. It was not long before he had acquainted them with the fact of his being a soldier's son, and from that he drifted into telling the story of "Father's button!" There was a roaring applause when he had finished.

"Here, Youngster," said one of the older men, holding out his pewter pot to him, "take a drink like a man. You deserve it!"

"No, thank you," the boy said. "I never drink beer."

Then, as an oldish-looking soldier, with a heavy moustache already tinged with gray, came up to him, Teddy turned to him in delight, "Are you Bouncer?"

"That's what I'm called."

The man's face was an unhappy one. He seemed to be the butt of his comrades, for they poured out such a volley of good-natured ridicule on his appearance that Teddy looked from one to the other in complete mystification.

"Will you come and see my home?" the child asked softly. "Corporal Saxby told me he thought you would like to come."

The man's face lightened. "Yes, that I will, if it isn't far off. My legs are that stiff and sore I don't want much walking."

"It isn't very far." Then, as they moved off together, Teddy slipped his little hand confidingly into the big one near him, and continued, "Do you know there's going to be a splendid tea for you all in our schoolroom tonight—have you heard?"

"Ay; the parson was round an hour ago giving out tickets. There's little to be done in a place like this. We are too tired to tramp into the town. So I expect there'll be a tidy few."

"The corporal came to tea at our house the other night. He is a friend of yours, isn't he?"

"The best friend I've got," was the hearty answer. "Yes, lad, there's few of his sort in the army. For one that tries to help us on a bit there are ten that try to drag us down!"

"I suppose," said Teddy dreamily, "that, after all, the Queen's army isn't so nice to be in as the army I belong to. Does your captain help you when you're in trouble?"

"He helps us to pack-drill, or C. B., or cells!" replied Tim Stokes with grim humour.

This needed to be explained to Teddy, who went on after it was made clear to him, "Ah! My Captain always helps me. Mr. Upton says when I do wicked things and get beaten by the enemy, I must call out to my Captain. He will come at once and help me."

"I reckon I've heard tell of your Captain, then, for that fellow Saxby is always pressing it into me. But I can't come to religion anyway—I can't make head or tail of it. I tell you, Youngster, I've been having an awful time lately. I can't keep to it. I'm certain the drink will do for me again. I can't keep away from it much longer. This march will see the end of my teetotal ways, I'm thinking."

"And won't my Captain help you?"

"I'm not a hand at prayers and Psalm-singing."

"I wish you would talk to Mr. Upton. He made me enlist a short time ago. I have been ever so much happier since I did it."

They were walking across the field leading to the farm, and as they came to the stile the soldier leaned heavily on it. Turning his face full on the child, he said determinedly, "I'm not going to talk to any Mr. Upton or anyone else about it. I would rather hear you than a parson. You remind me of a little brother of mine who died ten years ago. 'Tim,' he said, just before he went, 'Tim, will you meet me in heaven?' He was the only one I ever loved. I have lived a dog's life since!"

His eyes were moist with feeling, and for a minute Teddy looked at him silently in pitying wonder. Then he said, "Look here, Bouncer, this is what Mr. Upton said to me. He told me Jesus had died for me, and how dared I keep from being His soldier when He loved me so? You know that, don't you?"

"Yes, so Saxby tells me. But it doesn't make any difference."

"It didn't to me either," continued the boy eagerly, "until I went to God and enlisted. I did it quite by myself in the wood. You do it too, Bouncer—you give yourself to God as His soldier. He'll take you and keep you."

"I've been too bad. It keeps me awake at nights, the very thinking of it!"

"But won't God forgive you if you ask Him to?"

"Saxby says so, but I don't know. The fact is, a soldier can't be a Christian in the Army."

"I don't believe you want to be one of God's soldiers," said Teddy in a disappointed tone. "You keep making excuses!"

There was silence; then Tim Stokes heaved a heavy sigh.

"I won't come any further, Youngster. I'm not in a mind today to see company, but I'll be at the tea tonight."

"Oh, Bouncer, do come!" and Teddy's eyes filled with tears. "You promised you would. I do want you to see Mother and Granny!"

But Tim wheeled around and strode off with something like a sob in his throat. Teddy had little idea of the mighty conflict in his breast. The child's words had awakened many memories. Tim was at that stage now when the powers of good and of evil were contending for his soul.

"He don't believe I want it, for I keep making excuses!" muttered the poor man. "Ay, I do. I haven't got over the longing to be different. I would cut off my right hand, I do believe, if I could be as Saxby is. I can't bring myself up to the point; that's all!"

Meanwhile, poor little Teddy crept indoors with a sad face, to announce to his mother the failure of his mission.

"He was nearly here, Mother—just the other side of the hedge outside—and yet he turned back!"

CHAPTER VII

UPLIFTED AND CAST DOWN

It was a bright, cheery gathering a few hours later. Mr. Upton had thrown his whole heart into the scheme, and had been around with his tickets to a few outlying inns, where more of the men were billeted, so that there were altogether over forty redcoats assembled. Mrs. John and two other neighbours were in charge of the tea and coffee. Teddy and Nancy, with one or two other children, as a special favour, were allowed to help to wait on the guests. The tables were decorated with flowers. Meat-pies, cold beef, and ham sandwiches disappeared in a marvellous manner. The cakes and bread-and-butter with watercress were equally appreciated. Toward the end of the meal several ladies came forward and sang. One or two part-songs were also given by some of the guests staying at the Hall.

"Now," said Colonel Graham in his brisk, hearty tones, "before we have a few words from Mr. Upton, I should like to tell you how glad I am to see the redcoats around me once more. I know your regiment well, for my own, the 10th Hussars, lay with it in Gibraltar ten years ago. I am sure you have all enjoyed your tea, but perhaps you do not know who was the instigator of the whole thing. We must thank Mr. Upton for his untiring zeal and energy in making arrangements. We must thank the ladies for trying to make the evening pleasant by their songs. But we must thank a little man here, I am given to understand, for the proposal in the first instance."

And to Teddy's intense surprise the colonel swung him up on the impromptu platform, to receive a deafening round of applause.

He made a pretty picture as the light fell on his golden curls and sparkling blue eyes. His cheeks were flushed with excitement, but he bore himself bravely. He held his head erect as he faced the crowded room.

"He will speak to you better than I can," the colonel added, with a smile, "for I'm a poor speaker myself. I'm the old soldier here tonight, and my fighting days are past; his are all in the future. He looks forward to wear the red coat with the rest of you. I hope he'll bear as brave a part in the service as his father did before him. Now, my boy, have you anything to say?"

"It will turn his head," murmured Mrs. John to herself, but her mother's heart swelled with pride as his clear voice rang out, "It wasn't I who thought about the tea, it was Corporal Saxby (cheers). I haven't anything to say, unless you'd like me to tell you Father's story. I've told it once today, but you weren't all there. May I, Sir?"

"Certainly," was the colonel's amused reply. Teddy had never had such an audience before in his life, but he was quite equal to the occasion. Fingering his button, he began in his usual impetuous fashion. The very eagerness for his father's deed to be honoured prevented him from any feelings of self-consciousness. He carried his audience by storm.

The ladies were delighted and touched by it. Mrs. John quietly wiped some tears from her eyes.

And then Mr. Upton got up. His dreamy manner in speaking was absent now. He spoke straightly and forcibly to those in the Queen's service of the battle to be waged with sin. Touching on their special difficulties and temptations, he told them how absolutely impossible it was for them to be, in their own strength, a match for the devil with all the powers of evil at his back. He told them how the same Saviour who died for them, would keep them, and lead them on to certain victory, if they would but enlist in His service. Nothing could exceed the attention with which he was listened to, and the evening ended by their rising to their feet and singing "God Save the Queen." Then a sergeant rose to propose a vote of thanks. Cheers were given, and all departed, greatly pleased with their evening.

Teddy slipped up to Tim Stokes on going out.

"Shall I see you again?" he asked.

"I shall be busy tomorrow; we march out at eight in the morning."

"Oh, I shall come and see you off."

Tim lingered, then laying his hand heavily on the boy's fair curls, he said, "God bless you, little chap! I've done it."

Teddy's eyes lit up at once. "Have you—really and truly?"

He nodded. "My heart's full. I can't speak of it, but I was away near the woods there by myself before the tea. It's all right with me. I only wonder I didn't do it before. I wouldn't yield, that's the fact. Don't forget to pray for me, Youngster."

And he dashed out after his comrades, as if ashamed to show his emotion.

Teddy called his mother to him when in bed that night.

"Mother, I will be a soldier. I'm certain sure I will. I'm very glad I can be one of God's soldiers without waiting to grow up. And I think I shall be a recruiting sergeant for God now. I'm sure He wants lots more soldiers, doesn't He?"

"Indeed He does, my boy. Now go to sleep. You have had a very exciting day."

"But the best of all is," said Teddy sleepily, "that Bouncer has enlisted."

There was quite a crowd of villagers and children the next morning around the Hare and Hounds. The soldiers were drawn up outside, waiting for the approach of their regiment from the town to fall in and march on with them. Teddy and Nancy were there, of course. The little girl, in spite of her alleged disdain of soldiers, was delighted to be in their vicinity. Teddy could not get near his friend Bouncer, but he received a friendly nod from him in the distance. As for Bouncer's face, it was like sunshine itself, a marked contrast to the day before. As the band was heard approaching, cheers were given to the men now leaving. A tall corporal who had much enjoyed his tea the night before stooped to ask of Nancy, who was standing close to him, "What's the name of that curly-headed youngster who got us the tea?"

Nancy looked up at him mischievously: "The button-boy! That's what I call him. I shan't ever call him anything else!"

Then the corporal's voice rang out clear and loud: "Three cheers for the little button-boy!" which was taken up enthusiastically by the soldiers. Teddy hardly knew whether he was on his head or heels from excitement and delight. But he had to pay a penalty for his prominent position. From that day the title of the "button-boy" stuck to him. It became his nickname in the village by all who knew him.

On came the regiment, with the colours flying and the band playing in the most orthodox style. Teddy was bitterly disappointed when the warning bell of school prevented him from marching along the road with them.

The schoolmaster was very lenient with the boys that morning, or else they would have been in dire disgrace, for lessons were imperfectly learned and said. Never had he found it so difficult to keep their attention.

But if Teddy was inattentive and careless at school, he was doubly troublesome at home. For the next few days his mother's fears were realized. The excitement of all that had taken place seemed to have quite turned his head for the time. He jumped on Kate Brown's back—the hired girl—when she was carrying two pails of milk to the dairy, and the contents of both pails were spilt and wasted. He shut up a fighting bantam cock and the stable cat into a barn, and left them fighting furiously. He locked one of the farm-labourers in a hayloft, and pulled away the ladder, so that he was not released for hours. He proved such an imp of mischief in the house that even his mother meditated handing him over to his uncle to be whipped.

At last it came to a climax in school. He brought a lot of young frogs in a handkerchief. He put some of them in the master's desk. He amused himself at intervals by slipping the others down the backs of the boys seated in front of him. His corner was the most unruly one in the room. While waiting for another class to come down he began one of his stories in a whisper to a most interested audience.

"I went to see a goblin once that I heard of. He lived in a tub on the seashore. He lived by gobbling up schoolmasters and governesses. He used to cut their hair off, scrape them well like a horse-radish. Then he would begin at their toes and gobble them up until he got to their heads—their heads he boiled in a saucepan for soup. The boys and girls used to bring their masters, when they didn't . . ."

"Edward Platt!"

Never had the master's voice sounded so stern. The frogs were discovered! His wrath was not appeased by seeing the cluster of heads around Teddy, and catching a few words of the delicious story going on.

Teddy started to his feet.

"Who put these frogs here?"

"I did, Sir." The answer was boldly given.

"Come here!"

And amidst the sudden hush that fell on all the boys, Teddy walked up to the master's desk with hot cheeks and bent head.

"Edward Platt, for the last three days you have been incorrigible. I have kept you in, and given you extra tasks, but neither has had any effect. Now I shall have to do what I have never yet done to you. Hold out your hand."

Teddy's head was raised instantly, and holding himself erect he bore unflinchingly the three or four sharp strokes with the cane that the master thought fit to give him.

"Now," said the master, "you can go home. I will dispense with your attendance for the rest of this morning."

Teddy walked out without a word. He felt the disgrace keenly, but it was the means of bringing him to himself. Rushing away to a secluded corner in a field he flung himself down on the ground and sobbed as if his heart would break. Half an hour later his uncle, happening to pass through that field, came across him.

"Why, Ted, what is the matter?" he inquired as he lifted him to his feet.

Teddy's tear-stained face and quivering lips touched him so, that he sat down on a log of wood near, and drew him between his knees.

"Are you feeling bad—are you hurt?" was the next question; and then Teddy looked up, and in a solemn voice asked, "What does the Queen do when her soldiers are beaten instead of getting a victory?"

"I—I'm sure I don't know. I can't remember the time when we were beaten. I reckon she's sorry for them."

"Doesn't she turn them out of her army?"

"Why, no!"

"What does God do when His soldiers leave off fighting, and knock under to their enemy?"

"I reckon He's sorry too."

Dimly Jake Platt began to see the drift of the child's questions. Teddy shook his curly head mournfully.

"I'm sure He'll have to turn soldiers out of His army if they give up fighting, and let the banner drag in the dust, and just let the enemy do what they like with them. Why, I've done worse than that!"—Here he clenched his little fists and raised his voice excitedly— "I've gone with the enemy. I've joined Ipse. That's being a deserter. Now I shan't ever, ever be able to get back again!"

His uncle looked sorely puzzled.

"Why aren't you at school? What have you been doing?"

Teddy told him all in a despairing tone, adding, "I can't meet Mother—I've been caned. And—and I've disgraced my button!"

Here his tears burst out afresh.

"Look here," said his uncle slowly, "I won't say that you haven't been a bad boy—your mother herself has been in sore trouble about you this last day or two. But if we get a fall in the mud, it isn't much good stopping there. The only thing is to pick ourselves up again, get ourselves cleaned, and then start again and walk more carefully. Can't you do that?"

"I'm a deserter," sobbed the boy. "My Captain won't have me back. I've disgraced Him. I've disgraced my banner. I've disgraced my button!"

"Your Captain will pick you up, I think, if you ask Him. He'll clean you up first-rate, and set you on your legs again."

"Will He?" And hope once more began to dawn in the dim blue eyes.

"Of course He will. I'm not good at verses and such like, but I do remember this one: 'Though your sins be as scarlet, they shall be as white as snow.' Won't that one fit you?"

Teddy did not answer. He stood looking up wistfully into the blue sky, as if unconscious of his uncle's presence, and then he sighed. "I think I would rather be alone, Uncle Jake."

Jake left him without a word, and went home to prepare Mrs. John for what had happened.

She was much distressed, but, like a sensible woman, took the right view of the case.

"He wanted to be pulled up sharp. My poor boy! Is he much hurt?"

The caning was such a minor point of Teddy's grief that Jake confessed to knowing nothing about it. Mrs. Platt was inclined to be indignant with the schoolmaster.

"Such a tiny little chap as he is. So full of feeling and nerves—he shouldn't have done it."

Yet only that morning she had almost given him a sound whipping herself for one of his mad pranks!

Shortly after Teddy crept in, and shutting the door behind him, put his back against it.

"Mother, Granny," he said, "I've been an awful boy at school this morning. I'm in disgrace. I've been caned."

His tone was tragic, then he added slowly, "But I'm very sorry. I'm sorry I was so naughty at home. I'm going to start again, because my Captain has forgiven me."

And then Mrs. John did the wisest thing she could do. She asked no questions, but got some warm water and took him off to wash his face and hands. She saw the red marks across the little hand, but refrained from making much of it. After putting his curly head in order, she drew it to her shoulder, and putting her arms around him, she said, "My Sonny, Mother is so glad her little son feels his naughtiness. She has been praying much for him today. And now tell me all about it?"

CHAPTER VIII

IN THE CLOVER FIELD

"Please, Mrs. Platt, can I see Teddy?" It was Nancy who was standing at the farmhouse door one lovely Sunday evening.

"I think he is out in the clover field. Don't you be romping around with him now, for he has taken his Sunday book out, and is as quiet as can be." Old Mrs. Platt was the only one at home. She motioned with her hand where her little grandson would be found.

Nancy discovered him a few minutes later, lying full length in the sweet-scented clover, an open book before him. When he raised his face to hers, it wore his most angelic look.

"Hello! What have you come here for?" he asked.

"To talk to you," and, without more ado, Nancy squatted down beside him. "What are you doing?" she went on; "And what is your Sunday book?"

"It's the Pilgrim's Progress. I love it. Don't you? I haven't been reading it though for a long time. I've been having a beautiful make-up."

"Tell me," and Nancy's tone was eager. Teddy looked away to the purple hills in the distance, and beyond and above them to the soft evening sky, with its delicate fleecy clouds flitting by, and taking every imaginable form and shape as they did so.

The dreamy, far-away look came into his eyes as he said slowly, "It's a Sunday make-believe, quite one to myself. I have never told it to anyone. I can only tell it to myself out of doors, when it is still and quiet. Then I feel sometimes it's quite real!"

"Do tell me," pleaded Nancy coaxingly.

"Well, it's getting to heaven—after I'm there, you know."

Nancy's eyes grew big with awe.

"Shall I tell you how I begin it?"

She nodded, and Teddy, turning over on his side, brought forth another book—a New Testament.

Turning to an open page he began to read with great emphasis, "'And he carried me away in the spirit to a great and high mountain, and showed me that great city, the holy Jerusalem, descending out of heaven from God.'"

"That's the Bible," said Nancy.

"Yes; now listen. I'm lying here in this field; it's very, very still. I hear a little rustle behind. I don't look around, and then, flash! comes a beautiful white angel. Now he's standing in front of me."

"What's he like?"

"He's dressed in white, shiny stuff. He has very white, feathery wings. His face is smiling. He has eyes like mother's, and hair like Sally White's."

"'Flaxen,' Mother says it is," put in Nancy.

"Yes; he stands quite still. Hush! Hear him! 'Teddy, I've come to fetch you to heaven.' And then I stand up. I listen hard, but I don't say anything. He says, 'You haven't been altogether a good soldier, but the Captain says He wants you. Come along.' Then I get up and sit myself between his wings, and put my arms around his neck, and he begins to go up. I see Mother, and Granny, and Uncle Jake, and I wave my hand to them. Mother throws a kiss at me and calls out, 'Give my love to Father,' and away we go, over our fields and across the high road, and over Farmer Green's fields. Then we fly right to the top of that mountain over there!"

"Do let me come, too!" said Nancy. "I want to be on the angel's back with you."

"Perhaps you can follow behind on another angel. I want mine all to myself. We get up to the top of the mountain, then I stand down on the ground."

"And me, too!" put in Nancy.

"You must not keep stopping me. I can't feel it if you do. I stand there. I think at first I can't see nothing but a lot of little soft clouds, one above the other, just like those over there; but the angel says, 'Put your foot on one of them, and then on the next one—they are the steps to heaven!'"

"Oh!" gasped Nancy, following it with keen reality. "You'll tumble!"

"I don't. It's like putting your foot in cotton wool. I go up—I have to go quite by myself, but the angel comes behind, to see I don't fall. And then he says, 'Look up. Don't you see the gates?' And then I look, and I see them—shining golden gates, very big, and covered with jewels like Mrs. Graham wears on her fingers. I go up and up, and then I'm there."

"Is that all?"

"Why, that's just the beginning. I'm only outside. The gates are shut, but when they see me coming, two more angels come and swing them wide open. I'm feeling rather frightened, but I walk in. There's a long wide street made like the gates. I walk very carefully, for fear of slipping down. Then I see a lot of angels coming along with trumpets. They go first and begin to play like the soldiers' band. I march on to a very, very, very big door. There on the steps leading up stands my Captain."

Teddy paused. "I can't tell you what He's like, but I feel what He's like myself. Such a loving, kind face. He puts His hand on my head and says, 'Well done, Teddy!' And then I take hold of His hand. I think I cry."

Matter-of-fact Nancy sees with surprise that Teddy's eyes are filling with tears at the thought.

He went on softly, "I think He takes me up in His arms then, because I'm very tired. He carries me into the most beautiful garden you ever saw in your life. He takes me to my father, who is waiting there."

"Tell me what the garden's like."

Teddy does not speak. He is full of the meeting with his father. Nancy waits a little impatiently.

"The garden is lovely," he said at last, drawing in a breath of delight at the thought. "It's always sunny and warm. The grass is very soft and green. There's every flower in the world all bunched up together. The seats are made of roses. If you want to go to sleep, the pillows are made up of violets. There's a beautiful river, and trees full of apples and oranges, and plums and pears. The banks are red—they are made of strawberries."

"Oh!" gasped Nancy, "how lovely!"

"There are summer-houses, and little white boats to row on the river. There are golden harps hanging up on the trees. Then I think, I hope, there are lots of dogs running about. You can ride all day on lions, and tigers, and bears. They won't bite you, but lick your hands."

"Go on. What else?"

"Then we stand up and sing hymns when my Captain comes by. We play on the harps, and blow the trumpets as much as ever we like. I think my Captain sometimes comes and sits down and talks to us and tells us stories."

There was silence; then Nancy said, "Is that all?"

"That's enough for you," said Teddy, a little condescendingly. "I think and make believe a lot more."

"I want to go to heaven," Nancy said thoughtfully.

Then Teddy came back to earth.

"Have you enlisted yet?" he asked.

"I'm not going to be a soldier," said Nancy quickly.

"Well, you'll never get to heaven if you don't fight for our Captain now. He won't let you inside the gates unless you belong to Him. Girls can fight just as much as boys."

"Of course they can. I can fight as well as you, button-boy!"

"Why don't you fight your enemy, then?"

"What enemy?"

"My enemy is called Ipse. He's a dreadful trouble to me. You have got yours—the thing inside you that makes you want to do naughty things. You've got to fight it. Do the good things instead. I've had two fights with Ipse today."

"Have you? Do tell me!"

"You mustn't tell any one, then. It was in church this morning. There was an old woman in front of me. She'd untied her bonnet. The ribbons fell over in our pew. She went fast asleep in the sermon, and nodded her head back until it almost tumbled off her head. Ipse thought if I would put out my hand and just give a tiny, weeny pull at the ribbon, it would come right off!"

Nancy clapped her hands. "Why didn't you? What fun!"

"I wanted to let Ipse have his way dreadful, but I remembered I must fight him, and I did. I asked my

Captain to help me. Then I put both my hands in my pockets and screwed up my eyes tight. But I was glad when she woke up and tied her bonnet on again."

"That was much better than I could have done. What was the other fight you had?"

"Uncle Jake brought some fresh honey from the hives. He put it on a plate in the window in the kitchen. He'd said when he went out of the room, 'Don't touch that, Teddy,' as I was waiting for Mother to come to church with me. I went up and looked at it. Ipse said to me, 'Just put one finger in it.' And I had to fight him very hard over that, but I ran away out of the room."

"And do you always fight him hard?"

"No; I often forget until it's too late. Mother said I must ask my Captain to make me remember. I do ask Him a lot to help me."

"I don't think I like that sort of fighting."

"Nancy, I wish you would give yourself to God as His soldier." Teddy turned around earnestly as he spoke.

"I think," said Nancy slowly, "I like to be naughty best." Then she added, with a quick change of tone, "My father is coming home soon. He'll come to see us here. Then you'll see what a grand sailor he is. He is much grander than your father was."

"My father was an officer," said Teddy proudly.

"So's my father. He is a first-class petty officer," and Nancy brought out the words slowly and with much emphasis.

"My father was a non-commissioned officer," said Teddy, determining not to be beaten. "He was a full sergeant."

"My father gives orders to all the sailors, and they have to do what he tells them."

"So did my father. He led the soldiers through a battle."

"My father will fight in twenty battles before he dies. Yours only fought in one."

"My father is in heaven, and that's the grandest place to be in."

Coming to this climax was too much for Nancy, and the thoughts of that place of which they had been having so much talk subdued their rising ire.

Teddy said reproachfully, after a minute's silence, "Ipse was nearly getting angry with you then. You are such a dreadful girl for making me quarrel with you."

"You won't let me say my father is as good as yours," protested Nancy.

"He isn't better. Yes—don't get angry, Nancy; let's say they're just the same."

And with this admission Nancy was for the time pacified.

Before they parted she looked at her little companion with solemn eyes.

"I won't promise, but I'll think about belonging to the Captain. I should like to go to heaven."

It was one day soon after this that Teddy was straying over the fields in his happy, careless fashion. Fond as he was of games with the village boys, often there were times when he liked his own society best. He wandered on talking to himself, and gathering grass and wild flowers as he went. His quick eyes soon noted some sheep making their way through a gap in the hedge, and from there they were going through an open gate into the high road.

"Those are Farmer Green's sheep," he said to himself. "I'm glad of it—horrid old man he is! No, Ipse, be quiet; that isn't the way to think of him. I'll go and drive them back again!"

And he trotted off with this intention. But it is much more difficult to get sheep into their rightful place than out of it. This Teddy found to his cost. His face was hot and red, his voice hoarse with shouting. Then, to his consternation, Farmer Green appeared on the scene.

"You young vagabond!" he shouted, springing toward him, a thick stick in his hand. "Leave my sheep alone! How dare you come on my premises? You're always after some fresh trick or other."

Teddy stood still until he came up to him. Teddy looked up frankly at Farmer Green.

"Indeed, Sir, I was trying to drive them back through their hole again. Look, that's where they broke through."

"A likely story! Much more probable you made the hole yourself."

Teddy's blood rushed into his face. "I never tell a lie!" he cried, "and you are a . . ."

He stopped, and hung his head in shame at the word that almost slipped from him.

Jonathan Green looked curiously at him.

"Now may I ask what the end of that speech was going to be?" he said grimly.

Teddy looked up. "Ipse was going to say you were a liar yourself, but I just stopped him in time."

"I shall believe you have a bee in your bonnet, as some folks say," said the farmer. "If the sheep came out of their proper field, what business was that of yours?"

"I wanted to be good to you. I'm sorry I tied you up that day, dreadful sorry. And I've got to love you. So I thought it would be a good plan to send your sheep back again."

"You've got to love me!" repeated the farmer, opening his eyes in mock surprise. "And when did I ask for any of your love, young fellow?"

"I don't suppose you want me to," observed Teddy cheerfully, as he saw that the stick, instead of being brandished over his head, was now safely resting on the ground, "but I've got to do it, you see, because my banner I'm holding for my Captain is Love. And I must love everybody."

The farmer did not answer.

Teddy continued earnestly, "Do you think you could manage to forgive me, and let us shake hands? It would make it easier for me to love you if you could."

There was such honesty of purpose in the blue eyes raised to his, such wistful curves to the sensitive little lips, that Jonathan Green for the first time felt the thrall of the child's power.

"Come into the house with me," he said, "and I'll see what the missis has to say to you."

Teddy followed him without the slightest misgiving. He was led into the farmhouse kitchen, where Mrs. Green sat knitting over the fire. One of her daughters was laying the cloth for tea.

"Mary Ann, here's the scamp of the village come to see you. Keep him here till I come back. I'm after some stray sheep;" and shutting the door with a bang the farmer disappeared.

Teddy shook hands with the old lady and the young one, and then seated himself in the big chair opposite Mrs. Green.

"What have you been doing?" the latter inquired; "how is it your mother can't keep you out of mischief?"

"I haven't been in mischief. Really I haven't"; and poor Teddy felt the truth of the saying, "Give a dog a bad name and hang him."

He tried to tell his story, and then when that did not seem to be understood, he deftly changed the subject.

"What does Farmer Green like best in the world?" he asked.

This astonishing question struck Mrs. Green dumb, but her daughter Natty laughed.

"Gooseberry pudding!" she said. "Now then, what is the next question?"

But Teddy was silent, and not another word did he say until the farmer came in again.

"This youngster is on the tack of reforming himself, Mary Ann," said Jonathan, sitting down in the chair that Teddy immediately vacated upon his entrance. "Do you believe it?"

"I have no faith in boys," said Mrs. Green, with a shake of her head. "They're all alike, and are always taking you unawares!"

"You hear what the missis says. You won't get any help from that quarter. But I'll give you a chance. Would you like to have tea with us?"

Teddy smiled. "Thank you, Sir, but Mother will expect me home for tea. May I go now? And do you forgive me for what I did the other day?"

Farmer Green stretched out a rough hand, and took the boy's small one. "Here's my hand on it!" he said with his grim smile. "I may be a fool for believing you, but if you are sorry for the past, I won't be the one to rake it up."

Teddy's upward look was so full of innocence that he received a clap on the shoulder.

"Run along. You have made your peace with me."

And speeding away Teddy whispered to himself, "I shall ask Mother to make it. I shall pick the gooseberries myself. Then he'll know I love him!"

Farmer Green was very bewildered a few days after at receiving a parcel which was left at his house by some boys on their way back from school; he was still more puzzled when upon opening it. It proved to be a gooseberry pudding in a basin with a piece of paper attached to it with these words in very shaky writing,

I send you my love.
—Teddy.

But his daughter was able to enlighten him. They had a hearty laugh over Teddy's mode of confirming the truce of friendship.

CHAPTER IX

LOST

O ur little soldier had his ups and downs, but on the whole he was making steady progress, and his mother was thankful to see his increased thoughtfulness and gentleness. He was not less merry and joyous; he was still the leader of the village sports. But he was learning how to control his mischievous propensities and to restrain his hasty words and actions. Nancy was a great trial to him sometimes. Though the two were ceaselessly involved in arguments and differences, they could not keep apart for long. Nancy's father arrived. Teddy had the privilege of being invited to tea, and of hearing the most wonderful yarns from the big brown-bearded man, who, though outwardly rough in voice and manner, had a very soft corner in his heart for his little daughter.

Teddy listened and admired the sea stories and satisfied Nancy by his evident appreciation. But when he reached home, and was asked about his visit, he said emphatically, "Nancy's father is very nice, but he's nothing like the picture I've got of Father with his red coat and sash and sword. His voice is so gruff and hoarse. He shouts so loud. I shall never, never think sailors are better than soldiers!"

It was after Nancy's father had left, when the bright summer days were beginning to close, that one afternoon Teddy and Nancy were fishing together. At least that was their intention, but anyone seeing them sitting on the low stone bridge over the river, with their lines dangling carelessly in the water, and their merry laughter and voices ringing out continually, would not be surprised if their fishing did not meet with success. At last they clambered down and wandered along the tow-path. Suddenly Nancy drew Teddy's attention to his button.

"Why, it's nearly coming off; you'll lose it!" she cried.

"I told Mother it was getting loose yesterday. She says she is always sewing it on. I think I'll take it right off and put it in my pocket. What would I do if I were to lose it?"

He was jerking at it as he spoke, and it slipped from his grasp and rolled away on the path. It was too great a temptation for Nancy. Like lightning she was after it. A moment later stood upright and exultant, with the button clenched tightly in her little hand.

"Give it to me at once!" demanded Teddy, quivering all over with excitement.

Nancy's brown eyes sparkled with mischief. "Aha, little button-boy, I've got it at last. I shall take it home and have it sewed on my jacket."

"I shall fight you," cried Teddy, "if you don't give it up at once! It isn't yours. You would be a thief if you kept it. Give it to me this minute!"

"Shall I throw it into the river?" questioned the saucy little maiden.

Teddy darted forward, and then began a tussle. He tried to wrench her hands apart. She exerted all her strength to keep them closed. Suddenly, with a triumphant cry from Teddy, as Nancy's fingers were beginning to yield, the button was liberated with such force that it flew violently out. Splash! Into the river it went! Nancy gave a cry, but without a word or sound Teddy plunged in head foremost after it. It was done without a thought. He was a good swimmer, and for a minute Nancy watched him in breathless silence. But when his little head rose out of the water, he seemed half stupefied, and cried out in a weak voice, "Help! I'm drowning!" and then sank again. Nancy set up a shout of frantic agony then. A carter coming over the bridge fortunately heard her, and came to the rescue, not a moment too soon. He threw off his coat and heavy boots, and plunged in just as Teddy's curly head rose for the third and last time. It did not take long to bring him to shore, but he lay in the carter's arms limp and lifeless. Nancy burst into an agony of tears.

"He's dead! He's dead. I've killed him!" she cried.

The carter wasted no time in trying to restore animation to the little frame, but all his efforts were unavailing, and at last he said, "I'll put him in my cart, and drive as fast as I can to the doctor's. It isn't more than a mile off, if he is at home. You go home and fetch his mother as fast as you can."

Nancy raced off, sobbing as she went, and she was in such a state of excitement that when at length she burst open the farmhouse door she seemed to have lost her speech.

Mrs. John saw her face, and started forwards. "It's Teddy!" she cried. "What has happened?"

"He's at—he's going to the doctor's—dead!" she gasped, then fell breathless to the floor. Without a word Mrs. John snatched up a shawl. With white, set face, and lips moving in agonized prayer, she flew along the road to the doctor's. She was shown into the room where the doctor was hard at work. Teddy lay like a waxen image, with the sweetest smile on his lips, his fair curls clustering around his brow. Only an ugly bump amongst the curls told the reason of his sinking under the water again so suddenly.

In breathless silence the mother stood and watched. "Don't give him up, Doctor!" she cried, as at last the doctor straightened himself and paused, looking at the mother sorrowfully. He shook his head, but set to work again, trying artificial respiration, and leaving no effort untried to bring back the life that had apparently departed.

And then there came the moment when his efforts met with success, for placing his hand against the little heart he felt a feeble throb. He redoubled his efforts. The breath began to appear, a faint colour tinged the blue lips. At last the heavy eyelids raised, and a faint voice said, "Mother!"

Mrs. John sank on her knees. "Thank God!" was all she said. Then she fainted.

Much later in the evening, Teddy was placed in his own little bed at home. Though alive, his condition was most critical. He lay in a heavy stupor from which it seemed impossible to rouse him. The doctor said he must have struck his head against a stone when first he dived into the river. This had produced concussion of the brain. Nancy had been taken home before he came, but the news was brought to her that he was still alive, though in great danger. That was a great comfort to her poor little sorrowful soul.

For many days he lay between life and death. The inquiries after him from every one of his schoolfellows, the Hall, and the different farms and places around, told his mother how much her little son had been beloved. And when on the following Sunday Mr. Upton gave out, in a faltering voice, "The prayers of this congregation are desired for Edward Platt, who is very dangerously ill," there was not a dry eye in the church. One or two audible sobs came from the boys' seats in the gallery.

Mrs. John never left her boy's bedside—night and day she was by him. Many wondered at her calm peacefulness. After the first great shock, she had been able to hand over her child into her Father's loving hands, and rest content with the result. So she was able, in perhaps the most anxious time of her life, to look up and say, "Father, not my will, but Thine be done."

The days slowly passed and still no change for the better. The doctor came and went with his grave, impenetrable face. Teddy was still unconscious. Then doubts began to rise in his mother's heart as to whether his reason would ever come back. She stopped the doctor as he was leaving one morning to ask him a question. "If he lives, Doctor, will his brain be damaged? My brave, bonny boy!"

And the doctor could only give her the meagre consolation, "He may recover yet. I have seen worse cases than this pull through, and be as bright as ever they were."

And then, one afternoon, when the setting sun was flooding the room with a golden glory, the little head turned on the pillow. "Mother!"

The sound of that word, not uttered since she had seen him in the doctor's house that first terrible day, was like the sweetest music in her ear. Stooping over him she met the clear conscious gaze of the blue eyes.

"So tired, Mother! Put your hand under my cheek. Good-night."

The eyelids closed, and the limbs relaxed in healthy sleep. The mother sat down. Though her arm became stiff and weary, not a muscle of it moved.

The doctor came in just before he woke.

"He has spoken. He knew me," she said; and the doctor nodded and smiled. And then a minute later the boy raised his head.

"Where am I, Mother?" he asked feebly.

"In bed, Darling. You have been ill."

"Where's my button?"

"He'll do," said the doctor contentedly. "Keep him quiet, and feed him up."

And the glad news went around the village that Teddy was getting better.

It was a bright day for the farm when Teddy was brought down in a blanket and put in the big easy-chair by the fire. His little face and hands looked very fragile, with the blue veins standing out clearly under the transparent white skin. But his large eyes shone with light and gladness. His mother made him comfortable. Then she left him in his grandmother's charge for a short time. Old Mrs. Platt had had her share of suffering during those sad days. Her heart was wrapped up in the boy. Perhaps the greatest trial of all was to stand aloof, and perform her daily work downstairs, while her daughter-in-law had the sole charge of him.

She came across to the chair now. Kneeling down in front of it, said, with tears in her eyes, as she took his two little hands into hers, "Granny has sadly missed her pickle all this while."

And then Teddy put his little arms around her neck. He hugged her close, crushing her cap in the most reckless fashion as he did so.

"I'm getting better every day, Granny. I love you so much!"

When Mrs. Platt released herself, he went on more soberly, "I feel very tipsy on my legs. I asked Mother to let me walk just now, but I couldn't manage very well. I don't think I shall be able to run fast for a year, shall I?"

"Oh, we'll see you about long before that, please God!"

"And, Granny, you know about my sorrow?"

The blue eyes looked wistful at the thought.

"Yes, Laddie. Don't think of that now."

"I told Mother I didn't want ever to get well when I first talked about it. I felt I couldn't live without my button, but she told me that was wrong. She said it wasn't being a good soldier to wish to die when trouble came, and that if I bore my sorrow well God would be pleased. Do you think I'm bearing it well, Granny?"

"Yes, yes," Mrs. Platt said soothingly. "Look at those lovely flowers and grapes that Mrs. Graham sent to you this morning. Wasn't that kind of her?"

"I don't ever forget it," pursued Teddy, refusing to have the subject changed, "but I thought this morning that God could give it to me again. So I'm going to ask Him every day till it comes. Do you know, Granny, I think He'll give it to me. Only Mother says I must be patient."

Presently he asked, "Could I see Nancy, one day soon?"

"She comes on her way to school every day to ask how you are. Poor little maid! She's taken on dreadful about your illness. She wouldn't eat her food when you were so ill. Her mother got quite anxious about her. We will send for her in a day or two, if you keep well."

And two days after, Nancy appeared. She came up to the big chair very shyly, and looked with awe on Teddy's white, wasted face. Then she cried impulsively, "Oh, Button-boy, will you ever, ever forgive me? If you had died, it would have been me who killed you!"

"No, you wouldn't," said Teddy, putting up his face and kissing her. "I was just as naughty. I shouldn't have tried to fight with you."

"I go to the river every day," Nancy went on sorrowfully, "and Farmer Green brought a big net one day and dragged up a lot of stones and old tin pans, but the button wasn't there. I hope it will be washed ashore one day. So I look along the banks, but I haven't seen a sign of it yet!"

"I'm asking God to give it back to me every day," said Teddy, with a little decided nod. "I think He'll do it. You ask Him too, Nancy, and perhaps He'll do it quicker."

"I've asked God every day to make you better. I promised Him if He would do it I would be the Captain's soldier. Yes, I did. I said I would give up being a sailor, and be just a soldier, like you are."

Nancy made this statement with great solemnity, and Teddy beamed with delight.

"And are you really enlisted?"

"I don't quite know, but I am trying to be good. I ask Jesus to help me every day."

Then there was silence. Nancy sat down on the rug, and took the large tabby cat on her lap.

"Did you think you were going to die?" she asked presently.

"I didn't think anything at all until I woke up, and saw Mother crying over me. Then I felt dreadful tired and ill. I asked her one day where she would bury me, for I was sure I was much too ill to get better. She— well, she smiled, and said God was making me stronger every day. I didn't feel I was better a bit."

"Would you like to have died and gone to heaven?"

"Yes," Teddy answered promptly, "of course I would. Wouldn't you?"

Nancy shook her head. "I might if I was quite sure the angel would carry me safely all the way without dropping me, or leaving me in the clouds before we got there. I think I like to live here best. Besides, I don't think I'm good enough to go to heaven yet."

"I don't think it's being good gets us to heaven. Jesus died to let us, you know, like the hymn says—

Jesus loves me! He who died
Heaven's gate to open wide;
He will wash away my sin,
Let His little child come in.

"Have you asked Him to forgive you, Nancy?"

Nancy nodded. "Yes, when you were so ill. I felt I had been so wicked that God was punishing me."

Here, reverting to more earthly topics, Nancy held up the cat arrayed in her sailor hat and jacket.

"Look, this is Jack Tar! Doesn't she make a jolly sailor?"

A gleeful, hearty peal of laughter came from Teddy, and was heard in the adjoining room by his grandmother with comfort. She called Mrs. John.

"Hear that, now! Why, he's getting quite himself again. It does him good to have a child to talk to. She must come again."

And this Nancy did, and the roses began to come back to Teddy's cheeks. Others of his playfellows were allowed to come and see him.

Certainly no little invalid could have received greater attention than he did during that time of convalescence. Every day small offerings were presented at the door by the village children. Very diverse were the gifts. Sometimes a bunch of wild flowers. Sometimes birds' eggs, marbles, boxes of chalk, a packet of toffee or barley-sugar, a currant bun, a tin trumpet, a whistle, a jam tart, a penny pistol, and so on. His mother declared she would have to stop taking them in, as they were getting such an accumulation of them.

"And how is my little fellow-soldier?" asked Mr. Upton, as he came in one day for his first visit to the little invalid after being downstairs.

"He'll soon be out of hospital," responded Teddy brightly.

"And is he still fighting for his Captain?"

"I think, Sir, Ipse has been very good while I have been ill."

"He has been lying low, has he? If I mistake not, you will have a brush with him yet before long, so be on the look-out."

And Teddy found the good rector's words come true. Days came when he tried his mother's patience much by his fractiousness and restlessness. He was more often the vanquished than the conqueror.

Even Nancy one day remonstrated with him.

"You are nasty and cross today. No one pleases you."

"I want to get out. I'm tired of this old kitchen."

"If you can't get out, you can't. Being cross won't take you out." This logic convinced, but did not comfort. "I expect your Captain won't come near you when you're cross."

And then Teddy burst out crying, "I'm not a soldier at all. I don't know how to stand fire. It's all Ipse. I'm too tired to fight him!"

Poor little soldier! One above took note of the physical weakness and weariness, and in His tenderness pitied and forgave.

CHAPTER X

FOUND

It was winter time, and Teddy was back at school, full of health and spirits. Yet, through all his boyish mirth, the loss of his button was never forgotten. Daily he prayed for it to be found. His hope and faith in God never failed him.

"Perhaps God will send it to me for a Christmas surprise. Perhaps I shall find it in my stocking on Christmas morning," he used to say to his mother. She told him to pray on.

He had come in from school one cold day in the beginning of December. He was watching with keen interest the roasting of an apple suspended from a string in front of the fire, when there was a sharp knock at the door, and the footman from the Hall appeared.

"The master wants you to let the youngster come up with me now and speak to him."

"What about?" questioned Mrs. John, rather alarmed at this summons, and wondering if Teddy had been up to mischief.

"He won't keep him long." Then, as excited Teddy began pulling on his great-coat, the footman whispered something into Mrs. John's ear, which had the effect of completely reassuring her, and bringing a pleased smile about her lips. Teddy was delighted to go up to the Hall. He trotted along by the side of the tall, young footman, keeping up a brisk conversation as he went.

"I shall never be a footman," he was asserting. "I couldn't keep my legs so stiff. You are always like the soldiers when they stand at Attention. Don't you ever kick your legs out in the kitchen, or have you got stiff knees?"

"I can kick out as much as I like," responded the young man, in a rather offended tone.

"Don't you think it's nicer to be a soldier? Wouldn't you like to be one?"

"No. Their grub is something shocking. They live like cattle!"

Teddy would not allow this, and the discussion began to get somewhat heated, when their arrival at the house put an end to it.

"I say, just tell me, is the colonel angry?" asked Teddy, as looking into the large, brightly lighted hall, he suddenly felt his diminutive size.

"Not he. Wipe your feet, and take your cap off."

Teddy stepped in upon the soft rugs almost on tiptoe. The colonel himself came out into the hall to meet him. "Come in, my little man. Don't be frightened."

Teddy held his head erect as he followed the colonel into a bright, cheery room, where a group of ladies and gentlemen were around the fire enjoying their cup of five o'clock tea.

Mrs. Graham came forward and gave him a kindly greeting.

"This is our would-be soldier," said Colonel Graham—"the 'button-boy,'" as I hear he is called. Some of you remember his story told in our school-room to the regiment passing through in the summer. We were not surprised to hear of his narrow escape from death from trying to regain his button. But perhaps you have forgotten all about it, Youngster? A button isn't worth much sorrow after the first pang of its loss is over."

Teddy's face was a picture. The blood rushed up to his forehead. His eyes flashed. With clenched hands he said boldly, "Do you think I could ever forget my father's button, Sir? I would rather have it back than anything else in the world! And I'm going to get it back, too!"

"But it's at the bottom of the river, isn't it?"

"I don't know where it is, but God does. I ask Him every day to send it back to me. I'm quite sure He will. I think it will be this Christmas."

The ladies exchanged glances.

"Fact is stranger than fiction certainly," said the colonel. "Now, my boy, come here."

He was standing on the hearthrug with his back to the fire, and putting his hand into his pocket he drew out a small box and placed it in the child's hand.

"Open it, and tell me if you recognize the contents."

Teddy lifted the lid, and then a gasp and a cry of ecstasy broke from him.

"Oh, my button. My own button! Oh, Sir!"

And here the tears welled up in the blue eyes. Utterly regardless of the place he was in, he flung himself down on the hearthrug and buried his head, face foremost, in his arms. He lay there so still for a moment that Mrs. Graham bent forward to touch him, fearing that the excitement might be too much for him, but he was only trying to hide his emotion from those looking on. In another minute he rose to his feet, and with a face perfectly radiant he turned to the colonel, "It's lovely, Sir, it's lovely!"

The colonel had had it set in a little gold framework with blue ribbon attached, making it look as much like a medal as possible. Mrs. Graham now came forward and pinned it to his coat.

"Now, my boy, I don't think you will ever guess how it came into our possession. The other day I brought home a few fish. In preparing one of these for table, our cook discovered your button inside it—I wonder the fish had not come to an untimely end before from such an indigestible meal! She told us of it, not recognizing what a valuable treasure she had brought to light. When we saw it, we knew it was the redoubtable button that has been the means of causing such interest in our neighbourhood."

Teddy listened eagerly. "No wonder no one could find it!" he said, fingering his adornment proudly. "It's like the fish that brought Peter some money once."

Then the colonel turned to one of his friends. "Now, Major, what do you think of this youngster? Would you like to take him as a drummer boy into your regiment?"

The major scanned the boy from head to foot, then answered emphatically, "I wouldn't take a boy with a face like that for a good deal!"

"Why not?" asked Mrs. Graham.

"Because it's the ruination of them. I shall never forget a pretty boy we had once; he was called the 'cherub.' He had been a chorister—sang divinely. He was only four years in the regiment, and his case was brought to me before he was discharged. He came to us an angel, and departed a finished young blackguard. He drank, stole, and lied to any extent, and was as well versed in vicious sins as any old drunkard in the regiment. When I see a fresh drummer brought in, I wonder how long he will keep his innocence. Sometimes I wish his friends could see the life he is subjected to. I give them a month generally, and then away flies their bloom and all their home training."

"But, Major Tracy, you are giving us a shocking idea of the morals in the service," said one lady.

He shrugged his shoulders. "I grant you, on the whole, they are better than they were. But the service is no place for highly strung boys like this one. The rougher, harder natures get on best. When they get older, and have sense and strength enough to stick to their principles, then let them enlist."

"But I have always heard," said Mrs. Graham, "that the drummer boys are well looked after now. They have a room to themselves. The chaplains have classes for them."

"That may be. I would only ask you to watch a boy, as I have, from the start, and see what kind of a man he grows into after having spent most of his early youth in the service. There are exceptions, I know, but precious few, as far as my experience goes."

Teddy did not understand this conversation, but he gathered from the major's tone that he did not approve of him.

"Do you think I'm too small to be a soldier?" he asked.

The major laughed. "Don't bother your head about your size," he said. "You'll grow. There's plenty of time before you."

"I don't want to be a drummer," said Teddy earnestly. "I would rather wait and be a proper soldier—a soldier who fights."

"A capital decision—stick to it, little chap. You have my hearty approval."

"You have your father's blood in your veins," said the colonel, laughing. "Meanwhile, I suppose you try your hand on the village boys, to content your fighting propensities."

"No," said Teddy, a grave look coming into his sunny blue eyes. "I don't fight with anybody but Ipse now. He always keeps me busy."

"Who is Ipse?" asked Mrs. Graham.

"He's my own enemy. Mr. Upton told me about him. You see, I belong to God's army. He takes very little soldiers. I've been enlisted for months and months. Ipse is just another part of me—the bad part!"

There was silence on the little company for a minute, then Major Tracy said with a laugh, "What an original little oddity he is! —Quite a character!"

And then Teddy was dismissed. He flew down the avenue home as fast as he could. Snow was falling, but he heeded it not. He burst into the kitchen a little later in a breathless state of excitement.

His mother knew already, so was prepared for his news. However, she was not prepared for the handsome adornment now on her boy's coat. His grandmother and uncle were equally pleased and gratified at the colonel's kindness.

Teddy's prayer of thanksgiving that night touched his mother greatly.

"O God, I do thank You. I knew You would answer me. You knew how dreadful it was to live without my button. You knew how unhappy my heart was about it, though I tried to be brave, and not talk about it. Please, do help me to take great care of it, and never let me lose it again!"

The next morning before breakfast, Teddy ran off to tell Nancy, and to show her the long-lost treasure. She was quite as delighted as he was, but said, a few minutes later, "Button-boy, do you remember telling me you couldn't live without your button? You said you'd pine away and die."

"Yes, I thought I would. But as soon as I began to pray about it I knew it was coming back. So I got better."

"Well," said Nancy with a sigh, "I won't ever try to get your button again. But if you were to die before me, I wonder if you would let me have it then? I would take great care of it."

"I meant it to be buried with me," said Teddy, considering, "but I don't mind altering my mind about it. If you promise not to give it to anyone else, I will let you have it."

"I promise truly," vowed Nancy, "I told you I wouldn't love you until you gave it to me. But I will now, because I'm trying to be good!"

"And we'll always remember that soldiers and sailors are just as good as each other—they are quite even!"

"Yes," nodded Nancy. "Sailors and soldiers are quite even. My father is just as good as your father was!"

Teddy looked a little doubtful at this, but wisely refrained from making any objection to the assertion. They parted, Nancy calling out after him, "And when you die, and I get the button, I shall wear it as a brooch!"

"Mother," said Teddy, a few days after this, as she was paying him her usual "goodnight" visit, "It's a very funny thing. I used to wish for an enemy so much, to fight and carry on with. Now I've got one, and have Ipse to fight with. I'm getting rather tired of him. Is that wicked? I asked Mr. Upton today if I couldn't ever get rid of Ipse—I mean when I am grown up, but he said I never should altogether, but that I could keep him well under, so that he wouldn't trouble me so. He does trouble me a lot now."

"Soldiers must never get tired of fighting, Sonny. You have your Captain to help you."

"Yes. I suppose when I get bigger and stronger it will be much easier, won't it? Mother, do you have any fighting? Have you got an enemy like me?"

"Yes, indeed I have, my boy."

"But you are never beaten, are you? You never do anything wrong!"

"I don't get into mischief, and disobey orders, perhaps," Mrs. John said, smiling, "but I have lots of difficulties and temptations that you know little about, Sonny. I am afraid I very often get beaten by the enemy."

Teddy pondered over this. "When I get to heaven I shan't have to fight with Ipse, shall I?"

"No, Darling; there will be no fighting with sin there."

Teddy smiled. "Perhaps my Captain will think I've been nearly as brave as Father if I fight Ipse hard until I die."

"There is a verse in the Bible that says, 'He that ruleth his spirit is better than he that taketh a city.' Mother would rather have her little son fight God's battles than be the bravest soldier in the Queen's army."

"But," said Teddy, "I mean to do both. Now, Mother, just before I go to sleep, give me Father's button to kiss!"